Guitar Chord Songbook

2nd Edition

T0079000

The following songs are the property of:

Bourne Co.
Music Publishers
www.bournemusic.com

BABY MINE
GIVE A LITTLE WHISTLE
I'M WISHING
SOME DAY MY PRINCE WILL COME
WHEN YOU WISH UPON A STAR
WHISTLE WHILE YOU WORK
WHO'S AFRAID OF THE BIG BAD WOLF?

Disney Characters and Artwork © Disney

ISBN 978-1-5400-6108-9

HAL•LEONARD®

Visit Hal Leonard Online at
www.halleonard.com

Contact us:
Hal Leonard
7777 West Bluemound Road
Milwaukee, WI 53213
Email: info@halleonard.com

In Europe, contact:
Hal Leonard Europe Limited
42 Wigmore Street
Marylebone, London, W1U 2RN
Email: info@halleonardeurope.com

In Australia, contact:
Hal Leonard Australia Pty. Ltd.
4 Lentara Court
Cheltenham, Victoria, 3192 Australia
Email: info@halleonard.com.au

Guitar Chord Songbook

Contents

Alice in Wonderland

from ALICE IN WONDERLAND

Words by Bob Hilliard
Music by Sammy Fain

Melody:

Al - ice in Won-der- land.

G°7   G   D7   Am7   Em   F#7   Bm7   E7   D°7   A7

Verse 1

G°7 G D7 G
Al - ice in   Wonderland.

Am7   D7   G
How do you get to Wonderland?

Am7   D7   G   Em
Over the hill or under - land

   Am7   D7   G
Or just be - hind the tree?

Verse 2

G°7 G   D7 G
When clouds go   rolling by,

Am7   D7   G
They roll a - way and leave the sky.

Am7   D7   G   Em
Where is the land be - yond the eye

   F#7   Bm7 E7   Am7
That people cannot see?

     D7   G
Where can it be?

Bridge

Am7 D7 G
Where do   stars go?

Am7   D7   G
Where is the crescent moon?

   F#7   Bm7   E7
They must be some - where

         Am7   D7
In the sunny after - noon.

Verse 3

G°7 G D7 G   D°7
Al - ice in   Wonder - land.

Am7   D7   G
Where is the path to Wonderland?

Am7   D7   G   A7
Over the hill or here or there?

  Am7 D7 G
I won - der where.

Baby Mine
from DUMBO

Words by Ned Washington
Music by Frank Churchill

Melody:

Ba - by   mine,

(Capo 2nd fret)

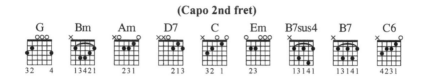

G   Bm   Am   D7   C   Em   B7sus4   B7   C6

Verse 1

G   Bm   Am   D7
Baby mine, don't you cry.

G   Bm   Am   D7
Baby mine, dry your eye.

C   Am
Rest your head close to my heart,

        D7   G   Em   Am   D7
Never to part, baby of mine.

Verse 2

```
G    Bm          Am              D7
Little  one, when you play,

G       Bm          Am              D7
Don't you mind what they say.

C                       Am
Let those eyes sparkle and shine,

        D7        G
Never a tear, baby of mine.
```

Bridge

```
Em                  B7sus4    B7
If they knew sweet little you,

Em                  B7sus4    B7
They'd end up loving you too.

Em                  Bm
All those same people who scold you,

Em                  Bm    Am D7
What they'd give just for the right to hold  you.
```

Verse 3

```
G       Bm          Am              D7
From your head to your toes,

G       Bm          Am              D7
You're so sweet, goodness knows,

C                   Am
You are so precious to me,

        D7        G
Cute as can be, baby of mine.

        Am   C6   G
Baby mine, baby mine.
```

The Ballad of Davy Crockett

from DAVY CROCKETT

Words by Tom Blackburn
Music by George Bruns

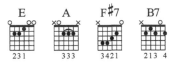

Verse 1

    E   A   E
Born on a mountaintop in Tennes - see,

                  F#7   B7
Greenest state in the Land of the Free.

    E   A
Raised in the woods so's he knew ev'ry tree,

    B7   E
Kilt him a b'ar when he was only three.

Chorus 1

    E   A   E
Davy, Davy Crockett,

    B7   E
King of the wild fron - tier!

Verse 2

    E   A   E
Fought single-handed through the Injun War

                   F#7   B7
'Till the Creeks was whipped and peace was in store.

      E   A
And while he was handlin' this risky chore,

    B7   E
Made his-self a legend forever - more.

Chorus 2

     E   A   E
Davy, Davy Crockett,

     B7   E
The man who don't know fear.

Verse 3

     E   A   E
He went off to Congress and he served a spell

                         F#7   B7
Fixin' up the government and laws as well.

     E   A
Took over Washington so we heard tell

     B7   E
And patched up the crack in the Liberty Bell.

Chorus 3

     E   A   E
Davy, Davy Crockett,

     B7   E
Seein' his duty clear.

Verse 4

     E   A   E
When he'd comes home, his poli - tickin' done,

                      F#7   B7
The western march had just begun.

             E   A   F#7
So he packed his gear and his trusty gun,

     B7   E
And lit out a grinnin' to follow the sun.

Chorus 4

     E   A   E
Davy, Davy Crockett,

     B7   E
Headin out West a - gain!

The Bare Necessities

from THE JUNGLE BOOK

Words and Music by
Terry Gilkyson

Melody:

Look for the

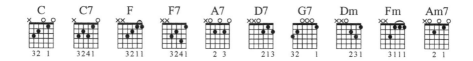

C	C7	F	F7	A7	D7	G7	Dm	Fm	Am7

Chorus 1

> N.C.   C   C7
> Look for the   bare ne - cessities,
>
>   F   F7
> The simple bare ne - cessities;
>
>   C   A7   D7   G7
> For - get about your worries and your strife.
>
>   C   C7
> I mean the   bare ne - cessities,
>
>   F   F7
> Or Mother Nature's recipes
>
>   C   A7   Dm   G7   C   F   C
> That bring the bare ne - cessities ___ of life.

Verse 1

N.C.   G7
Wherever I wander,

         C
Wherever I roam,

        G7
I couldn't be fonder

       C   C7
Of my big home.

          F   Fm
The bees are buzzin' in the tree

            C   D7
To make some honey just for me.

    Am   N.C.   A7 N.C.
When you   look under the rocks and plants

    Dm N.C.   Dm   G7
And take a glance at the fancy ants,

     C   A7
Then maybe try a few.

N.C.   Dm
The bare ne - cessities

 G7   C   A7   Dm
Of life will come to you,

     G7   C   F   C
They'll come to you.

Chorus 2

N.C.   C   C7
Look for the   bare ne - cessities,

    F   F7
The simple bare ne - cessities;

    C   A7   D7   G7
For - get about your worries and your strife.

     C   C7
I mean the   bare ne - cessities,

    F   F7
That's why a bear can rest at ease

    C   A7   Dm   G7 C F C
With just the bare ne - cessities ___ of life.

Verse 2

N.C.   G7
Now when you pick a paw-paw

             C
Or a prickly pear;

           G7
And you prick a raw paw,

            C   C7
Next time be - ware.

                F   Fm
Don't pick the prickly pear by the paw,

              C   D7
When you pick a pear, try to use the claw.

    Am N.C.   A7 N.C.
But you   don't need to use the claw

      Dm N.C.   Dm   G7   C
When you pick a pear of the big paw-paw.

             A7
Have I given you a clue?

N.C.   Dm
The bare ne - cessities

  G7   C   A7   Dm
Of life will come to you,

    G7   C   F   C   N.C.
They'll come to you.

Tuba Solo

C	C7	F	F7	
C	A7	D7	G7	
C	C7	F	F7	
C A7	Dm G7	C F	C N.C.	

Piano Solo   *Repeat Tuba Solo*

Trumpet Solo	C	C7	F	F7	
	C	A7	D7	G7	
	C	C7	F	F7	
	C A7	Dm G7	C N.C.	C N.C.	

Verse 3

G7
So just try and   relax, yeah. Cool it.

C
Fall apart in my backyard

G7
'Cause let me tell ya somethin', Little Britches,

If you act like that bee acts,

C   C7
Uh, ah, you're workin' too hard.

F   Fm
And don't spend your time just lookin' a - round

C   D7
For somethin' you want that can't be found.

Am   N.C.   A7   N.C.
When you   find out you can live   without it

Dm   N.C.   Dm   G7
And go a - long not thinkin' about it.

C   A7
I'll tell you somethin' true.

N.C.   Dm   G7
The bare ne - cessities of life

C   F   C   F   C   Dm
Will come to you,

G7   C   F   C
Mow - gli, how 'bout you sing.

Chorus 3

N.C.   C   C7
Look for the   bare ne - cessities,

   F   F7
The simple bare ne - cessities;

   C   A7   D7   G7
For - get about your worries and your strife.

      C   C7
I mean the   bare ne - cessities,

   F   F7
That's why a bear can rest at ease

   C   A7   Dm   G7   C   A7   Dm   G7
With just the bare ne - cessities ___ of life.

   C   A7   Dm   G7   C   N.C.
With just the bare ne - cessities ___ of life.

Be Our Guest

from BEAUTY AND THE BEAST

Music by Alan Menken
Lyrics by Howard Ashman

Melody:

Be our guest! Be our

G   Gmaj7   G6   G#°7   Am7   D7   Am   Am(maj7)   A#°7   Bm7   Bb7

G7   C   B7   Em   A7   E7   B°7   A   A°7   D7sus4

Verse 1

     G   Gmaj7
Be our guest! Be our guest!
    G6   G
Put our service to the test.
         G#°7
Tie your napkin 'round your neck, cherie,
   Am7   D7
And we'll provide the rest.
      Am   Am(maj7)
Soup du - jour! Hot hors d'oeuvres!
    Am7   D7
Why, we only live to serve.
    Am7   A#°7
Try the grey stuff. It's de - licious!
      Bm7   Bb7   Am7
Don't be - lieve me? Ask the dishes!
D7   G   Gmaj7
They can sing! They can dance!
     G6   G
After all, Miss, this is France!
            G7   C
And a dinner here is never second best.
        B7
Go on, un - fold your menu.
     Em   A7   Am7
Take a glance and then you'll be our guest,
    D7   G
Oui, our guest. Be our guest!

Verse 2

            G   Gmaj7
Beef ra - gout! Cheese souf - flé!

  G6   G
Pie and pudding "en flam - bé!"

                        G$\sharp$°7
We'll prepare and serve with flair

  Am7   D7
A culi - nary caba - ret.

          Am   Am(maj7)
You're a - lone and you're scared,

   Am7   D7
But the banquet's all pre - pared.

      Am7   A$\sharp$°7
No one's gloomy or com - plaining

      Bm7   B♭7   Am7
While the flatware's enter - taining.

D7   G   Gmaj7   G6   G
We tell jokes. I do tricks with my fellow candle - sticks.

                    G7   C
And it's all in perfect taste. That you can bet!

          B7
Come on and lift your glass.

                Em   A7   Am7
You've won your own free pass to be our guest.

        D7   Bm7   E7
If you're stressed it's fine dining we sug - gest.

    Am7   D7   G
Be our guest! Be our guest! Be our guest!

Bridge

Em   B7
Life is so unnerving for a servant who's not serving.

        B°7   A
He's not whole without a soul to wait up - on.

A°7   Em
Ah, those good old days when we were useful.

Am7   B7
Suddenly, those good old days are gone.

        Em   B7
Ten years we've been rusting, needing so much more than dusting.

        B°7   A
Needing exercise, a chance to use our skills.

A°7   Em
Most days we just lay around the castle.

Am7   D7
Flabby fat and lazy. You walked in, and oopsadaisy!

Verse 3

      G   Gmaj7
It's a guest! It's a guest!

         G6   G
Sakes a - live, well, I'll be blessed.

                                $G\sharp°7$
Wine's been poured, and thank the Lord,

         Am7   D7
I've had the napkins freshly pressed.

         Am   Am(maj7)
With des - sert she'll want tea.

        Am7   D7
And, my dear, that's fine with me.

        Am7 $A\sharp°7$
While the cups do their soft-shoeing

      Bm7   B♭7 Am7
I'll be bubbling! I'll be brewing!

D7   G   Gmaj7
I'll get warm, piping hot.

        G6   G
Heaven sakes! Is that a spot? Clean it up…

        G7   C
We want the company im - pressed!

        B7
We've got a lot to do.

        Em   A7   Am7
Is it one lump or two for you, our guest?

        D7   Am7   D7
She's our guest! She's our guest! She's our guest!

Verse 4

G   Gmaj7
Be our guest! Be our guest!

      G6   G
Our com - mand is your re - quest.

                  G#°7   Am7
It's ten years since we had anybody here,

         D7
And we're ob - sessed!

      Am   Am(maj7)
With your meal, with your ease,

   Am7   D7
Yes, in - deed, we aim to please.

      Am7   A#°7
While the candlelight's still glowing,

   Bm7   Bb7   Am7
Let us help you, we'll keep going

D7   G   Gmaj7
Course by course, one by one!

    G6   G
'Til you shout, "Enough, I'm done!"

                G7   C
Then we'll sing you off to sleep as you di - gest.

     B7
Tonight you'll prop your feet up!

    Em7   A7
But for now, let's eat up!

    Am7   Bm7   Am7
Be our guest! Be our guest! Be our guest!

    D7sus4 D7 G
Please, be   our guest!

Beauty and the Beast
from BEAUTY AND THE BEAST

Music by Alan Menken
Lyrics by Howard Ashman

Melody:

Tale as old as time,

(Capo 1st fret)

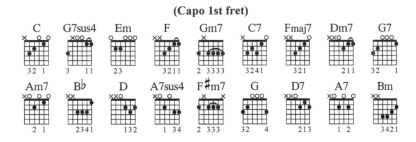

C   G7sus4   Em   F   Gm7   C7   Fmaj7   Dm7   G7

Am7   B♭   D   A7sus4   F♯m7   G   D7   A7   Bm

Intro   ‖: C |G7sus4 |C |G7sus4 :‖

Verse 1

C   G7sus4   C
Tale as old as time,

          G7sus4   C
True as it can be.

          Em
Barely even friends,

          F   G7sus4 C
Then somebody bends unexpected - ly.

          G7sus4   C
Just a little change.

          Gm7
Small, to say the least.

C7   Fmaj7
Both a little scared,

          Em   Dm7
Neither one pre - pared.

G7   C   G7sus4
Beauty and the Beast.

Bridge

Em   F
Ever just the same,

         Em   F
Ever a sur - prise.

         Em
Ever as be - fore,

        Am7   B♭   C
Ever just as sure as the sun will rise.

Verse 2

D   A7sus4   D
  Tale as old as time,

          A7sus4   D
Tune as old as song.

         F♯m7
Bittersweet and strange,

         G
Finding you can change,

         A7sus4   D
Learning you were wrong.

         A7sus4   D
Certain as the sun

         Am7
Rising in the East,

D7   G
Tale as old as time,

         Em
Song as old as rhyme.

A7   D   Bm
Beauty and the Beast.

         G
Tale as old as time,

         Em
Song as old as rhyme.

A7   D
Beauty and the Beast.

A7sus4   D   A7sus4   D

Bella Notte
from LADY AND THE TRAMP

Music and Lyrics by
Peggy Lee and Sonny Burke

(Capo 3rd fret)

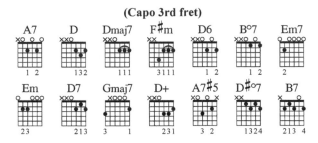

Verse

    A7 D   **Dmaj7**   **F#m**   **D6**
Oh, this is the night, it's a beau - tiful night,

        D **B°7 Em7**   **A7**
And we call it Bella Notte.

Em   **Em7**   **A7**
Look at the skies, they have stars in their eyes

    Em7 A7   **D**
On this lovely Bella Notte.

D7
Side by side with your loved one,

    Gmaj7 D+   **Gmaj7**
You'll find en - chantment here.

    Em   **A7**
The night will weave its magic spell

     Em7   **A7**
When the one you love is near.

A7#5 D   **D#°7**   **B7**
For   this is the night and heavens are right

    Em7 A7 D6
On this lovely Bella Notte.

Bibbidi-Bobbidi-Boo

(The Magic Song)

from CINDARELLA

Words by Jerry Livingston
Music by Mack David and Al Hoffman

Melody:

Sa - la - ga - doo - la, men-chic - ka boo - la,

(Capo 1st fret)

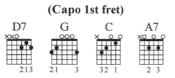

D7   G   C   A7

Intro | D7 | | G | ||

Verse 1

G
Salagadoola, menchicka boola, bibbidi - bobbidi - boo.
D7
Put 'em together and what have you got?
          G
Bibbidi - bobbidi - boo.

Verse 2

G
Salagadoola, menchicka boola, bibbidi - bobbidi - boo.
D7
It'll do magic believe it or not,
          G
Bibbidi - bobbidi - boo.

Bridge

          C   G
Now, salagadoola mean, menchicka boole - roo,
     A7   D7
But the thingamabob that does the job is bibbidi - bobbidi - boo.

Outro

G
Salagadoola, menchicka boola, bibbidi - bobbidi - boo.
D7
Put 'em together and what have you got?

                                    G
Bibbidi - bobbidi - bibbidi - bobbidi, bibbidi - bobbidi - boo.

Can You Feel the Love Tonight

from THE LION KING

Music by Elton John
Lyrics by Tim Rice

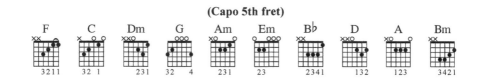

(Capo 5th fret)

Verse 1

      F   C
I can see what's happ'ning,

         F   C
And they don't have a clue.

           F   C
They'll fall in love and here's the bottom line,

         Dm   G
Our trio's down to two.

        F   C
The sweet caress of twilight,

          F   C
There's magic ev'ry - where.

        F   Am Em F
And with all this ro - man - tic   atmosphere,

        Bb   G
Dis - aster's in the air.

Chorus 1

         C   G   Am   F   C
Can you feel the love to - night,

                  F   G
The peace the evening brings?

        F   C   Am   F
The world for once in perfect harmony

      Dm F   G
With all its living things.

Verse 2

        F   C
So many things to tell her,

        F   C
But how to make her see

        F   C
The truth about my past.

               Dm   G
Impossible!   She'd turn away from me.

        F   C
He's holding back. He's hiding.

        F   C
But what? I can't de - cide.

        F   Am
Why won't he be the king I know he is,

        B♭   G
The king I see in - side?

Chorus 2   *Repeat Chorus 1*

Chorus 3
        D   **A**   **Bm** **G**   **D**
        Can you feel the love to - night?

                G   **A**   **G**
        You needn't look too far.

            D   **Bm**   **G**
        Stealing through the night's un - certainties,

        Em   **G**   **A**
        Love is where they are.

Chorus 4
           D **A**   **Bm** **G**   **D**
        And if he falls in love to - night,

          G   **A**   **G**
        It can be as - sumed

              D   **Bm** **G**
        His carefree days with us are history.

         Em   **A**   **G**   **D**
        In short, our pal is doomed.

Chim Chim Cher-ee
from MARY POPPINS

Words and Music by
Richard M. Sherman and Robert B. Sherman

Melody:

Chim chim - in - ey,   chim chim - in - ey,

(Capo 3rd fret)

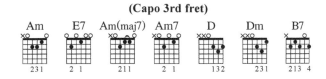

| Am | E7 | Am(maj7) | Am7 | D | Dm | B7 |

Intro |Am |E7 |Am |E7   ‖

Chorus 1

    Am   Am(maj7)   Am7   D
Chim chiminey, chim chiminey, chim chim cher - ee!

    Dm   Am   B7   E7
A sweep is as lucky as lucky can be.

    Am   Am(maj7)   Am7   D
Chim chiminey, chim chiminey, chim chim cher - oo!

        Dm   Am   E7   Am
Good luck will rub off when I shakes 'ands with you.

        Dm   Am   E7
Or blow me a kiss   and that's lucky…

Interlude |Am |E7 |Am |E7   ‖
    Too.

Verse 1

Am   Am(maj7) Am7   D
Now, as the ladder of   life 'as been strung,

    Dm   Am   B7   E7
You might think a sweep's on the bottom-most rung.

         Am   Am(maj7) Am7   D
Though I spends me time in the ashes and smoke,

  Dm   Am   E7   Am
In this 'ole wide world there's no 'appier bloke.

Chorus 2

Am   Am(maj7)   Am7   D
Chim chiminey, chim chiminey, chim chim cher - ee!

 Dm   Am   B7   E7
A sweep is as lucky as lucky can be.

Am   Am(maj7)   Am7   D
Chim chiminey, chim chiminey, chim chim cher - oo!

    Dm   Am   E7   Am
Good luck will rub off when I shakes 'ands with you.

Chorus 3

Am   Am(maj7)   Am7   D
Chim chiminey, chim chiminey, chim chim cher - ee!

 Dm   Am   B7   E7
A sweep is as lucky as lucky can be.

Am   Am(maj7)   Am7   D
Chim chiminey, chim chiminey, chim chim cher - oo!

    Dm   Am   E7   Am
Good luck will rub off when I shakes 'ands with you.

| Dm | Am | E7 | Am | ‖

Verse 2

```
Am          Am(maj7)  Am7     D
I choose me bristles with pride, yes I do.

Dm           Am        B7          E7
A broom for the shaft, and a brush for the flue.

|Am        |Am(maj7) |Am7       |D        |
|Dm        |Am       |E7        |Am       ||
```

Verse 3

```
Am          Am(maj7)  Am7        D
Up where the smoke is all billowed and curled,

      Dm           Am        B7          E7
'Tween pavement and stars is the chimney sweep world.

      Am                Am(maj7)  Am7    D
When there's hardly no day      an' 'ardly no night,

      Dm           Am        E7             Am
There's things half in shadow an' 'alfway in white.

      Dm        Am        E7         Am
On the rooftops of London,     ooh, what a sight!
```

Chorus 4

```
Am          Am(maj7)     Am7            D
Chim chiminey, chim chiminey, chim chim cher - ee!

      Dm          Am          B7          E7
When you're with a sweep, you're in glad compa - ny.

Am          Am(maj7)   Am7  D
Nowhere is there a more 'appier crew

      Dm            Am          E7             Am
Than them what sings, "Chim chim cher - ee, chim cher - oo."

Dm          Am          E7          Am
Chim chiminey, chim chim cher - ee, chim cher - oo.
```

Candle on the Water

from PETE'S DRAGON

Words and Music by
Al Kasha and Joel Hirschhorn

Melody:

I'll be your can-dle on the wa - ter,

C   G   F   G7   Dm   Am   Bb   E   C7

Gsus4   Fsus4   Gm7   Am7   D7   Em   Bbsus2   Fm   F#m7b5

Intro

‖: C   G |F   G7   :‖

Verse 1

C   Dm   F   G   C
I'll be your candle on the water,

            Am   Bb   G
My love for you will always burn.

            E   Am   C7
I know you're lost and drifting,

F   C
But the clouds are lifting,

F   C   Gsus4   G
Don't give up; you have somewhere to turn.

Verse 2

C   Dm   F   G   C
I'll be your candle on the water,

            Am   Bb   G
'Til ev'ry wave is warm and bright,

            E   Am   C7
My soul is there be - side you,

F   C
Let this candle guide you,

F   C   Gsus4   G
Soon you'll see a golden stream of light.

Bridge

Bb   C7   Fsus4   F   Bb
A cold and friendless tide has found you,

           C7   F   Gm7   F   Am7
Don't let the stormy darkness pull you   down.

         D7   Gsus4   G
I'll paint a ray of hope a - round   you,

F   Em   F   Bbsus2   G7
Circling the air,   lighted by a prayer.

Verse 2

C   Dm   F   G   C
I'll be your candle on the water,

         Am   Bb   G
This flame in - side of me will grow.

     E   Am   C7
Keep holding on, you'll make it,

F   C
Here's my hand, so take it,

F   G7   C
Look for me reaching out to show

   F   Fm   C   F#m7b5   F
As sure as rivers flow.

   Gsus4   G   C   G   F
I'll never let you go,

   G7   C   G   F
I'll never let you go,

   G7   C   G   F   C G7 C
I'll never let you go.

Circle of Life
from THE LION KING

Music by Elton John
Lyrics by Tim Rice

From the day we ar-rive on the plan - et

(Capo 3rd fret)

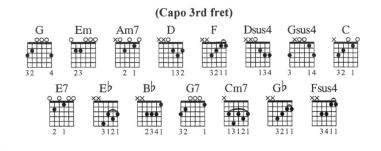

Intro

| G | Em | Am7 | D | |

| G | Em | Am7 | D |

Verse 1

           G   Am7
From the day we arrive on the plan - et

     D   G
And blinking, step into the sun,

       Em   Am7
There's more to see than can ever be seen;

      F   Dsus4   D
More to do than can ever be done.

Verse 2

            G   Am7
There's far too much to take in here;

     D   G
More to find than can ever be found.

       Em   Am7
But the sun rolling high through the sapphire sky

       F   D
Keeps great and small on the endless round.

Chorus 1

                                G   **Gsus4 G**
It's the circle of life,

                     F
And it moves us all.

                            C
Through despair and hope,

                    Dsus4   **D**
Through faith and love.

                     G   **E7**
Till we find our place

                            Am7   E♭
On the path un - winding

                  G   **Dsus4**
In the circle,

                  D   **C**   **G**
The circle of life.

Flute Solo   *Repeat Verses 1 & 2*

Chorus 2

                                  G   **Gsus4 G**
It's the circle of life,

                     F
And it moves us all.

                            C
Through despair and hope,

                          Dsus4   **D**
Through faith and love.

                    B♭   **G7**
Till we find our place

                         Cm7   G♭
On the path un - winding

                B♭   **Fsus4**
In the circle,

              F   E♭   B♭
The circle of life.

Colors of the Wind
from POCAHONTAS

Music by Alan Menken
Lyrics by Stephen Schwartz

Melody:

You think I'm an ig-no-rant sav-age,

(Capo 1st fret)

Cm   Bb   Ab   Gm   G7   C

Am   Em   F   G7sus4   G   Dm

Intro

| Cm |

    Cm   **Bb**
You think I'm an ignorant savage,

          Cm
And you've been so many places,

 Bb
I guess it must be so.

   Ab   **Gm**   **Ab**   **Gm**
But still I cannot see, if the savage one is me,

    Cm   **Ab**   **G7**
How can there be so much that you don't know?

N.C.   **C**   **Am**   **C**   **Am**
You don't know…

Verse 1

         C   **Am**
You think you own whatever land you land on.

         C   **Em**
The earth is just a dead thing you can claim.

   Am   **F**
But I know ev'ry rock and tree and creature

    G7sus4   **Am**
Has a life, has a spirit, has a name.

Verse 2

        C   Am
You think the only people who are people

            C   Em
Are the people who look and think like you,

        Am   F
But if you walk in the footsteps of a stranger

            G7sus4   C
You'll learn things you never knew you never knew.

Chorus 1

            Am   Em   F
Have you ever heard the wolf cry to the blue corn moon,

        Am   Em
Or asked the grinning bobcat why he grinned?

         F   G   C   Am
Can you sing with all the voices of the mountain?

         F   G7sus4
Can you paint with all the colors of the wind?

         F   G7sus4   C   Am   C   Am
Can you paint with all the colors of the wind?

Verse 3

         C   Am
Come run the hidden pine trails of the forest,

         C   Em
Come taste the sun-sweet berries of the earth.

        Am   F
Come roll in all the riches all a - round you,

        G7sus4   Am
And for once never wonder what they're worth.

Verse 4

        C   Am
The rainstorm and the river are my brothers.

        C   Em
The heron and the otter are my friends.

      Am   F
And we are all connected to each other

      Dm   G7sus4   C
In a circle, in a hoop that never ends.

Bridge

Em F   C   Am
How high does the sycamore grow?

      Bb   F   G   F
If you cut it down, then you'll never know.

Chorus 2

G   Am   Em   F
And you'll never hear the wolf cry to the blue corn moon,

      Am   Em
For whether we are white or copper-skinned,

           F   G   C   Am
We need to sing with all the voices of the mountain,

         F   G
Need to paint with all the colors of the wind.

      Dm   G   Em
You can own the earth and still all you'll own is earth

      F   Am   F   C   Am
Un - til you can paint with all the colors of the wind.

| F | G | C | | ‖ |

A Dream Is a Wish Your Heart Makes

from CINDERELLA

Music by Mack David and Al Hoffman
Lyrics by Jerry Livingston

Melody:

A dream   is   a   wish   your heart   makes ____

(Capo 3rd fret)

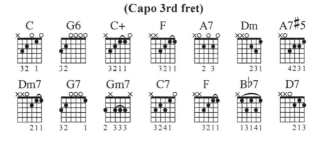

Verse 1

        C   G6   C
A dream is a wish your heart makes

            C+   F   A7
When you're fast a - sleep.

      Dm   A7#5 Dm7
In dreams you will lose your heartaches,

      G7   C   C+ Dm7 G7
What - ever you wish for, you keep.

      C   G6   C
Have faith in your dreams and someday

      Gm7   C7   F
Your rainbow will come smiling through.

      Dm   Bb7
No matter how your heart is grieving,

      C   D7
If you keep on be - lieving,

      Dm7   G7   C
The dream that you wish will come true.

A Cover Is Not the Book

from MARY POPPINS RETURNS

Music by Marc Shaiman
Lyrics by Scott Wittman and Marc Shaiman

Melody:

Un - cle Gu-ten-berg was a book - worm ＿

(Capo 1st fret)

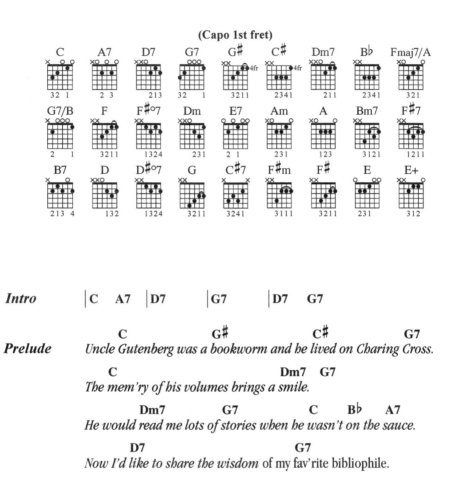

Intro | C   A7 | D7 | G7 | D7   G7

Prelude

        C   G#   C#   G7
Uncle Gutenberg was a bookworm and he lived on Charing Cross.

     C   Dm7   G7
The mem'ry of his volumes brings a smile.

      Dm7   G7   C   Bb   A7
He would read me lots of stories when he wasn't on the sauce.

      D7   G7
Now I'd like to share the wisdom of my fav'rite bibliophile.

Chorus 1

      Fmaj7/A G7/B C   **N.C.**
He said,   a   cover is not the book,

      D7
So open it up and take a look,

      G7   **C**
'Cause under the covers, one discovers that the king may be a crook.

      F   **F♯°7**   **C**   **B♭**   **A7**
Chapter titles are like signs, and if you read be - tween the lines,

    Dm   **N.C.**   **E7**   **N.C.**   **Am** **D7**
You'll find your first im - pression was mis - took,

    C   **N.C.**   **G7**   **N.C.**
For a cover is nice, but a cover is not the book!

Interlude 1

   C   **Dm7 G7**   **C**
Ta-ru-ra-lee ta - ra-ta-ta-ta!

    Dm7 G7   **C**
Ta-ru-ra-lee-ta - ra-ta-ta-ta.

      Dm7 G7   **C**   **Dm7**
Mary Poppins can   you give us an example?

  G7   **C**   **Dm7 G7**
Certainly.

Verse 1

   C   **A7**
"Nellie Rubina" was made of wood,

    D7   **G7**
But what could not be seen was, though her trunk up top was barren,

    C
Well, her roots were lush and green.

    F   **F♯°7**   **C**   **A7**
So in spring, when Mister Hick'ry saw her blossoms growing there,

    D7   **N.C.**   **G7**   **N.C.**   **D7**   **G7** **C**
He took root de - spite her bark and now there's seedlings ev'ry - where!

Chorus 2

       Fmaj7/A G7/B C
Which proves   a   cover is not the book,

      D7
So open it up and take a look,

       G7   **C**
'Cause under the covers, one discovers that the king may be a crook.

     F   **F#°7**   **C**   **B♭**   **A7**
Chapter titles are like signs, and if you read be - tween the lines,

    Dm   **N.C.**   **E7**   **N.C.**   **Am**   **D7**
You'll find your first im - pression was mis - took,

N.C. C   **N.C.**   **G7**   **N.C.**
For a cover is nice, but a cover is not the book!

Interlude 2

C Dm7 G7   **C**   **Dm7**   **G7**
Shall we do the one about the "Wealthy Widow?"

    A   **Bm7**   **E7**
Oh, by all means! I always loved that one.

    A   **Bm7**
Oh, go on then.

Verse 2

   E7 A   **F#7**   **B7**
"Lady Hyacinth Ma - caw" brought all her treasures to a reef,

     E7   **A**   **N.C.**
Where she only wore a smile, plus two feathers *and a leaf.*

   D   **D#°7**   **A**   **F#7**
So no one tried to rob her, 'cause she barely wore a stitch,

      B7   **E7**
For when you're in your birthday suit,

      B7   **E7**   **A**
There ain't much there to show you're rich!

Chorus 3

           A   F#7   B7
Oh, a cover is not the book, so open it up and take a look,

                  E7   A
'Cause under the covers, one discovers that the king may be a crook.

        D   D#°7   A   G   F#7
Ta-ru-ra-lee. Ta-ru-ra-la. Ta-ru-ra-lee. Ta-ra-ta-ta!

        Bm7   N.C.   C#7   N.C.   F#m
You'll find your first im - pression was mis - took,

        B7   A   N.C.
Ya, da, da, da, for a cover is nice,

        E7   N.C.
But a cover is not the book!

Interlude 3

      A Bm7 E7   A   Bm7   E7   A
Oh, give us the one about the "Dirty Rascal," why don't you?

        Bm7
Isn't that one a bit long?

E7   A   Bm7   E7
Well, the quicker you're into it, the quicker you're out of it.

| N.C. | A | F#   C#7 | F# | ‖ |

Rap

Once upon a time in a nursery rhyme,

There was a castle with a king hiding in a wing,

'Cause he never went to school to learn a single thing.

He had scepters and swords and a parliament of lords,

But on the inside he was sad, egad!

Because he never had a wisdom for numbers, a wisdom for words.

Though his crown was quite immense, his brain was smaller than a bird's.

So the queen of the nation made a royal proclamation,

"To the missus and the messers, the more or lessers,

Bring me all the land's professors."

Then she went to the hairdressers.

And they came from the East, and they came from the South.

From each college, they poured knowledge from their brains into his mouth.

But the king couldn't learn, so each professor met their fate,

For the queen had their heads removed and placed upon the gate.

And on that date, I state, their wives all got a note:

Their mate was now the late great!

But, then suddenly one day, a stranger started in to sing.

He said, "I'm the Dirty Rascal, and I'm here to teach the king!"

And the queen clutched her jewels, for she hated royal fools,

But this fool had some rules they really ought to teach in schools,

Like, "You'll be a happy king if you enjoy the things you've got.

You should never try to be the kind of person you're not."

So they sang and they laughed, for the king had found a friend,

And they ran onto a rainbow for the story's perfect end.

So the moral is, you mustn't let the outside be the guide,

For it's not so cut and dried,

Well, unless it's Doctor Jekyll, then you better hide… Petrified!

No, the truth can't be denied, as I have now testified:

All that really counts and matters is the special stuff inside.

Interlude 4 |E |F#°7 |C |E

Outro-   A   F#7   B7
Chorus   Oh, a cover is not the book, so open it up and take a look,

                          E7   A
               'Cause under the covers, one discovers that the king may be a crook.

                          D   D#°7   A   G   F#7
               So, please listen to what we've said, and open a book to - night in bed.

                  Bm7   C#7   F#m
               So one more time, be - fore we get the hook!

                          B7   A   E+
               Sing it out strong: A cover is nice. Please take our advice,

                  A   E+
               A cover is nice. Or you'll pay the price!

                  A   E7   A   F A F A F A
               A cover is nice, but a cover is not the book!

Evermore

from BEAUTY AND THE BEAST

Music by Alan Menken
Lyrics by Tim Rice

I was the one _ who had it all;

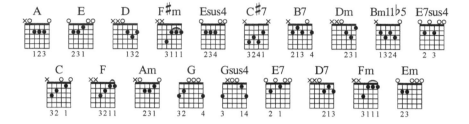

Verse 1

        A   **E**   **A**
I was the one who had it all;

        E   **A**   **D**
I was the master of my fate.

        F#m **E**   **F#m**   **D**
I never needed any - body in my life;

        A   **Esus4 E A**
I learned the truth too late.

          E   **A**   **E A**
I'll never shake a - way the pain.

            D   **A D**
I close my eyes, but she's still there.

    F#m   **E**   **F#m**   **D**
I let her steal into my melancholy heart;

        A   **E**   **D E**
It's more than I can bear.

Chorus 1

D   A
Now I know she'll never leave me,

D   A
Even as she runs a - way.

D   C#7
She will still tor - ment me,

F#m   A
Calm me, hurt me,

B7   E
Move me, come what may.

D   A
Wasting in my lonely tower,

D   C#7 F#m Dm   A
Waiting by an open door,

                           Bm11♭5   E7sus4
I'll fool myself she'll walk right in,

                  E   A
And be with me forever - more.

Verse 2

C
 I rage against the trials of love.

                     F
I curse the fading of the light.

                Am   G   Am   F
Though she's al - ready flown so far beyond my reach,

              C   Gsus4   G
She's never out of sight.

Chorus 2

```
         F              C
Now I know she'll never leave me,

F                  C
Even as she fades from view.

F            E7
She will still in - spire me,

Am  C     D7        G
Be a  part of ev'rything I do.

F                  C
Wasting in my lonely tower,

F            E7   Am  Fm
Waiting by an open door,

                        C      Dm
I'll fool myself she'll walk right in,

        Em               Am    F
And as the long, long nights be - gin,

          Em           Am   D
I'll think of all that might have been,

        C        Gsus4  G C   Am   F   G  C
Waiting here for - ever    -  more.
```

Friend Like Me

from ALADDIN

Music by Alan Menken
Lyrics by Howard Ashman

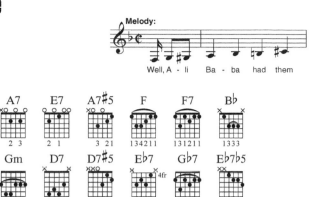

Intro

‖: **Dm** | **B♭7** **A7** :‖ *Play 3 times*
| **B♭7** N.C. **A7** | **Dm**

Verse 1

         A7   **Dm**
Well, Ali Baba had them forty thieves.

         A7   **Dm**
Schehera - zade had a thousand tales.

         A7   **Dm**
But, master, you in luck 'cause up your sleeves

         E7   **A7♯5**
You got a brand of magic never fails.

         A7   **Dm**
You got some power in your corner now,

         A7   **Dm**
Some heavy ammunition in your camp.

         A7   **Dm**
You got some punch, pizazz, ya - hoo and how.

         E7   **A7**
See, all you gotta do is rub that lamp.

N.C.   **A7**
And I'll say...

DISNEY

Chorus 1

Dm   Bb7 A7
Mister A - laddin sir,

    Dm   Bb7   A7
What will your pleasure be?

        F   F7   Bb   Db7
Let me take your order, jot it down.

        F   A7#5   Dm
You ain't never had a friend like me.

  Bb7 A7#5 Dm
No, no, no.

         Bb7   A7
Life is your restau - raunt

 Dm   Bb7
And I'm your maître d'.

       F   F7   Bb   Bbm
C'- mon whisper what it is you want.

       F   A7   Dm
You ain't never had a friend like me.

      Bb7
Yes, sir, we pride ourselves on service.

      Dm   A7   Dm
You're the boss, the king, the shah.

   Bb7
Say what you wish. It's yours!

              Gm   A7   Dm
True dish how 'bout a little more bakla - va?

         Bb7   A7
Have some of column "A".

   Dm   Bb7   A7
Try all of column "B".

    F   F7   Bb   Db7
I'm in the mood to help you, dude,

      F   A7#5   Dm Bb7 A7
You ain't never had a friend like me.

Interlude

Dm   Bb7 A7
Waahah. Oh my.

Dm   Bb7 A7
Waahah. No, no.

Dm   Bb7   A7 Bb7 A7
Waahah. Nana - na.

Bridge

Dm
    Can your friends do this? Can your friends do that?
                F7   A7
Can your friends pull this out their little hat?
             Dm   F
Can your friends go poof! *Well, looky here*.
                A7
Can your friends go abracadabra, let 'er rip
                   D7
And then make the sucker disap - pear?

Verse 2

          D7   Gm
So doncha sit there slack-jawed, buggy-eyed.
        D7   Gm
I'm here to answer all your midday prayers.
        D7   Gm
You got me bona fide certified.
        A7   D7$\sharp$5
You got a genie for your chargé d'af - faires.
      D7   Gm
I got a powerful urge to help you out.
        D7   Gm
So whatcha wish I really want to know.
        D7   Gm
You got a list that's three miles long no doubt.
        A7   D7
Well, all you gotta do is rub like so. And oh.

Outro

Gm   E♭7 D7
   Mister A - laddin sir,
        Gm   E♭7   D7
Have a wish or two or three.
    B♭   B♭7   E♭7   G♭7
I'm on the job, you big na - bob.
     B♭
You ain't never had a friend, never had a friend,
      G♭7
You ain't never had a friend, never had a friend,
      E♭7♭5   D7   Gm E♭7 D7
You ain't never had a friend like me.
Gm   E♭7 D7 Gm   E♭7   D7
Waahah.   Waahah.
      E♭7   D7 Gm
You ain't never had a friend like me. *Ha!*

Give a Little Whistle
from PINOCCHIO

Words by Ned Washington
Music by Leigh Harline

Melody:

When you get in trou-ble

G D7 Bm Em F°7 F♯ F♯7 E Am

Verse 1

     G   D7   G
When you get in trouble and you don't know right from wrong:
         D7   G
Give a little whistle, *Whistle*. Give a little whistle. *Whistle*.

Verse 2

     G   D7   G
When you meet temp - tation and the urge is very strong:
         D7   G
Give a little whistle, *Whistle*. Give a little whistle. *Whistle*.

Bridge

     Bm   Em   F°7   F♯   F♯7
Not just a little squeak; pucker up and blow.
                              Bm E   D7
And if your whistle's weak; yell, "Jiminy Cricket."

Verse 3

     G   D7   G
Take the straight and narrow path and if you start to slide;
         D7   E
Give a little whistle, *Whistle*. Give a little whistle. *Whistle*.
       Am   D7   G
And always let your conscience be your guide.

How Does a Moment Last Forever

from BEAUTY AND THE BEAST

Music by Alan Menken
Lyrics by Tim Rice

Melody:

How _ does a mo-ment last for - ev - er?

(Capo 1st fret)

Intro

| A Amaj7 | F#m A | Amaj7 | F#m A ||

Verse 1

```
         A              E          F#m    Amaj7
How does a moment last for - ever?

D                          A
How can a story never die?

      Esus4          E          A
It is love   we must hold on to;

      F#m   B7          E7sus4   E7
Never easy,        but we try.
```

Verse 2

```
         A              E          F#m    Amaj7
Sometimes our happiness is captured;

D                                  A
Somehow, a time and place stand still.

Bm               C#m    F#m
Love lives on in - side our hearts

      G#m   C#7
And always will.
```

Chorus 1

F#m   Bm
Minutes turn to hours;

Esus4   C#7 F#m Dm
Days to years, then gone.

     A   E   A   F#m
But when all else has been for - gotten,

Bm   E7sus4 E7 A   E   F#m   E
Still our song   lives on.

Verse 3

C   Cmaj7   Am   C
Maybe some moments weren't so perfect;

F   C
Maybe some mem'ries not so sweet.

     Gsus4 G   C
But we have to know some bad times,

     Am   D7   Dm7   G7
Or our lives are incom - plete.

Verse 4

C   Cmaj7   Am   C
Then, when the shadows over - take us;

F   C
Just when we feel all hope is gone,

     Dm   Em   Am
We'll hear our song and know once more,

     Bm   E
Our love lives on.

Interlude

F	C	Dm	Am Em	
			Ah, _____	
F	C	Dm	Am Em	
Oh, _____		oh. _____		
C Cmaj7	Am C	‖		

Verse 5

    C   Cmaj7   Am   C
How does a moment last for - ever?

    F   C
How does our happiness en - dure?

           Gsus4 G   C
Through the darkest of our troubles,

        Am   D7   Dm7 G7
Love is beauty, love is pure.

Verse 6

    C   Cmaj7   Am   C
Love pays no mind to deso - lation;

     F   C
It flows like a river through the soul,

     Dm   Em   Am
Pro - tects, proceeds and perse - veres,

     Bm   E
And makes us whole.

Outro-Chorus

    Am   Dm
Minutes turn to hours;

    Gsus4   E7 Am   Fm
Days to years then gone.

       C   G   C   Am
But when all else has been for - gotten,

    Dm   Gsus4 G Am   Fm
Still our song   lives on.

    C   G   C   Am
How does a moment last for - ever?

    Dm   Gsus4 G   C
When our song   lives on.

God Help the Outcasts

from THE HUNCHBACK OF NOTRE DAME

Music by Alan Menken
Lyrics by Stephen Schwartz

Melody:

I don't know if You can hear me

(Capo 4th fret)

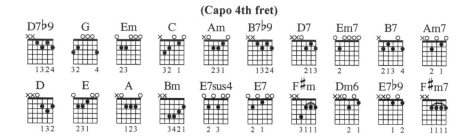

Verse 1

   D7♭9   G
I don't know if You can hear me

   D7♭9   G
Or if You're even there.

Em   C
I don't know if You would listen

Am   G
To a Gypsy's prayer.

Em   Am
Yes, I know I'm just an outcast,

 B7♭9   Em
I shouldn't speak to You.

D7♭9   G
Still, I see Your face and wonder

D7♭9   G D7♭9 G D7♭9
Were You once an outcast too?

Chorus 1

G   C
God help the outcasts, hungry from birth.

Am   D7   G
Show them the mercy they don't find on earth.

Em   Am
God help my people, we look to You still.

D7♭9   G   D7♭9 G
God help the outcasts or nobody will.

Verse 2

D7♭9   G   D7♭9   Em   Em7
 I ask for wealth.   I ask for fame.

         C   D7   G   B7
I ask for glory to shine on my name.

       Em   Em7   C   Em
I ask for love   I can pos - sess.

        Am   Am7   D   E
I ask for God and His angels to bless me.

Chorus 2

A   Bm
I ask for nothing. I can get by,

  E7sus4   E7   A
But I know so many less lucky than I.

F♯m   Bm
Please help my people, the poor and down - trod.

Dm6   A   E7♭9   F♯m
I thought we all were the children of God.

E7♭9   A F♯m E7♭9   A
God help the out - casts, children of God.

Outro

| E7♭9 | A | E7♭9 | F♯m | |
| F♯m7 | D | E | A | ‖ |

Hakuna Matata

from THE LION KING

Music by Elton John
Lyrics by Tim Rice

F   C   D7   G7   E7   Am   D   G   Bb   Eb

Chorus 1

N.C.   F   C
Timon: Hakuna ma - tata…what a wonderful phrase!

                  F   D7   G7
Pumbaa: Hakuna ma - tata… ain't no passing craze.

           E7   Am   F   D
Timon: It means no worries for the rest of your days.

                         C   G
Timon & Pumbaa: It's our problem-free phi - losophy.

      N.C.   C
Timon: Hakuna ma - tata

Verse

                 Bb   F   C
Timon: Why, when he was a young wart - hog…

         Bb   F   C
Pumbaa: When I was a young wart - hog!

N.C.
Timon: Very nice. Pumbaa: Thanks.

       Eb   F
Timon: He found his aroma lacked a certain appeal.

       C   G
He could clear the savannah after ev'ry meal!

      Bb   F   C
Pumbaa: I'm a sensitive soul,   though I seem thick - skinned.

   Eb   F   G
And it hurt that my friends never stood down wind!

Chorus 2

                           N.C.   F   C

Timon & Pumbaa: Hakuna ma - tata…what a wonderful phrase!

                                     F   D7   G

Pumbaa: Hakuna ma - tata… ain't no passing craze.

                      E7   Am   F   D

Simba: It means no worries for the rest of your days.

                                  C   G

Timon & Simba: It's our problem-free phi - losophy.

N.C.   C

  Hakuna ma - tata.

                            F   G   N.C.

All: Hakuna matata. Ha - kuna matata. Ha - kuna matata.

                     Am   F   D

Simba: It means no worries for the rest of your days.

                                  C   G

Timon & Simba: It's our problem-free phi - losophy.

N.C.   C   F

  Hakuna ma - tata. Hakuna ma - tata.

Outro

              G   C   F

‖: Hakuna ma - tata. Hakuna ma - tata. :‖ ***Repeat and fade***

He's a Tramp

from LADY AND THE TRAMP

Words and Music by
Peggy Lee and Sonny Burke

Melody:

He's a tramp, but they love him; ____

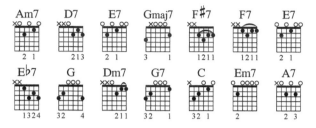

Am7	D7	E7	Gmaj7	F#7	F7	E7

Eb7	G	Dm7	G7	C	Em7	A7

Verse 1

       Am7 D7   **Am7**   **D7**
He's a tramp,   but they love him.

        Am7   **E7**   **Am7**   **D7**
Breaks a new heart   ev'ry - day.

       Gmaj7 F#7   **F7**   **E7**
He's a tramp,   they a - dore him

      Eb7   **D7**   **G**   **E7**
And I only hope he'll stay that way.

Verse 2

       Am7 D7   **Am7**   **D7**
He's a tramp,   he's a scoundrel,

       Am7   **E7**   **Am7**   **D7**
He's a rounder,   he's a cad,

       Gmaj7 F#7   **F7**   **E7**
He's a tramp,   but I love him.

      Eb7   **D7**   **G**
Yes, even I have got it pretty bad.

Bridge

        Dm7 G7   Dm7   G7   C
You can never tell when he'll show up.

        G7   C   Em7
He gives you plenty of trouble.

        A7   Em7   A7 Am7
I guess he's just a no 'count pup.

    E7   Am7   D7
But I wish that he were double.

Verse 3

       Am7 D7   Am7   D7
He's a tramp,   he's a rover

        Am7   E7   Am7 D7
And there's nothing more to say.

      Gmaj7 F#7   F7   E7
If he's a tramp,   he's a good one

    Eb7   D7   G   E7
And I wish that I could travel his way.

Eb7   D7   G   E7
Wish that I could travel his way,

Eb7   D7   G
Wish that I could travel his way.

How Far I'll Go

from MOANA

Music and Lyrics by
Lin-Manuel Miranda

Melody:

I've been _ star - ing at the edge of the wa - ter _

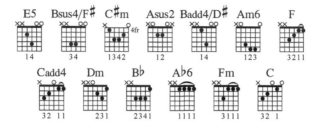

E5   Bsus4/F♯   C♯m   Asus2   Badd4/D♯   Am6   F

Cadd4   Dm   B♭   A♭6   Fm   C

Verse 1

     E5   Bsus4/F♯   C♯m

I've been staring at the edge of the water long as I can re - member,

             Asus2

Never really know - ing why.

     E5   Bsus4/F♯   C♯m

I wish I could be the perfect daughter, but I come back to the water,

             Asus2

No matter how hard I try.

      C♯m

Ev'ry turn I take, ev'ry trail I track,

      Badd4/D♯

Ev'ry path I make, ev'ry road leads back

       E5

To the place I know where I cannot go,

        Am6

Where I long to be.

Chorus 1

E5
See the line where the sky meets the sea?

Bsus4/F#
It calls me.

C#m   Asus2
And no one knows how far it goes.

E5   Bsus4/F#
If the wind in my sail on the sea stays behind me,

C#m
One day I'll know.

Am6
If I go, there's just no telling how far I'll go.

Verse 2

E5   Bsus4/F#   C#m
I know ev'rybody on this island seems so happy on this island.

Asus2
Ev'rything is by de - sign.

E5   Bsus4/F#   C#m
I know ev'rybody on this island has a role on this island,

Asus2
So maybe I can roll with mine.

C#m
I can lead with pride, I can make us strong,

Badd4/D#
I'll be satisfied if I play along.

E5
But the voice inside sings a diff'rent song.

Am6
What is wrong with me?

Chorus 2

        E5
See the light as it shines on the sea?

        Bsus4/F♯
It's blind - ing.

        C♯m   **Asus2**
But no one knows how deep it goes.

        E5
And it seems like it's calling out to me,

        Bsus4/F♯
So come find me

        C♯m
And let me know.

        Am6
What's be - yond that line? Will I cross that line?

Chorus 3

        F
See the line where the sky meets the sea?

        Cadd4
It calls me.

        Dm   **B♭**
And no one knows how far it goes.

        F   **Cadd4**
If the wind in my sail on the sea stays behind me,

        Dm   **A♭6**   **Fm B♭ C**
One day I'll know how far I'll go.

I See the Light

from TANGLED

Music by Alan Menken
Lyrics by Glenn Slater

All those days, watch-ing from the win-dows.

(Capo 3rd fret)

A   E7   D   E   B7   E7sus4   C#m   F#m   C#7

G7   C   F   D7   G7sus4   Em   Am   G

Intro |A | | | ||

Verse 1

      A   E7   A
All those days, watching from the windows.

              E7   A
All those years, outside, looking in.

      D   A   D   E
All that time, never even know - ing

      A   B7   E7sus4   E7
Just how blind I've been.

      A   E7   A
Now I'm here, blinking in the starlight.

             E7   A
Now I'm here, suddenly I see.

      D   C#m
Standing here, it's, oh, so clear

      F#m   B7   E7sus4   E7
I'm where I'm meant to be.

Chorus 1

```
       D          A
And at last I see the light,

         E7              A
And it's like the fog has lifted.

       D          A
And at last I see the light,

         C#7         F#m
And it's like the sky is new.

          D               A
And it's warm and real and bright,

          C#m                 D
And the world has somehow shifted.

A        E7            A
All at once, ev'rything looks diff'rent,

D     E7   A
Now that I  see  you.
```

Oboe Solo

```
|A     |E7  A  |          |E7        A  |
|D     |A   D E |A   B7   |E7sus4  E7  |G7       ||
```

Verse 2

```
C              G7          C
All those days, chasing down a daydream.

           G7      C
All those years living in a blur.

F             C        F   G7
All that time, never truly see - ing

C    D7          G7sus4   G7
Things    the way they were.

C              G7          C
Now, she's here, shining in the starlight.

           G7      C
Now she's here, suddenly I know.

F             Em
If she's here, it's crystal clear

    Am       D7     G7sus4   G7
I'm where I'm meant to go.
```

Chorus 2

```
                   F          C
        And at last I see the light,

               G7          C
        And it's like the fog has lifted.

               F          C
        And at last I see the light,

               E7           Am
        And it's like the sky is new.

               F              C
        And it's warm and real and bright,

               Em               G    F
        And the world has somehow shift - ed.

        C        G7        C
        All at once, ev'ryting is diff'rent,

        F      G7   C       Am  D7
        Now that I see you,

        G7sus4   G7   C
        Now  that  I  see you.
```

I'm Wishing
from SNOW WHITE AND THE SEVEN DWARFS

Words by Larry Morey
Music by Frank Churchill

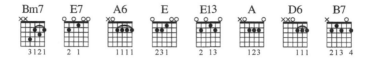

Prelude

> **Bm7**   **E7**
> Want to know a secret?
>
> **Bm7**   **E7**
> Promise not to tell?
>
> **Bm7**   **E7**   **A6**
> We are standing by a wishing well.
>
> **E**
> Make a wish into the well,
>
>   **Bm7**
> That's all you have to do.
>
>   **E**
> And if you hear it echoing,
>
>   **E7**
> Your wish will soon come true.

Verse 1

>   **A6**
> I'm wishing (I'm wishing)
>
> **Bm7**   **E7**
> For the one I love
>
>   **E13**
> To find me (To find me)
>
>   **A6**
> To - day. (Today.)

Verse 2

A6
I'm hoping (I'm hoping)

Bm7   E7
And I'm dreaming of

E13
The nice things (The nice things)

A6
He'll say. (He'll say.)

Interlude

A
Ah ah ah ah ah, (Ah ah ah ah ah,)

D6
Ah ah ah ah ah, (Ah ah ah ah ah,)

B7
Ah ah ah ah ah, (Ah ah ah ah ah,)

E
Ah ah ah ah ah ah ah ah ah.

Verse 3

A6
I'm wishing (I'm wishing)

Bm7   E7
For the one I love

E13
To find me (To find me)

A6
To - day. (Today!)

If I Never Knew You (End Title)

from POCAHONTAS

Music by Alan Menken
Lyrics by Stephen Schwartz

Melody:

If I nev-er knew you,

(Capo 3rd fret)

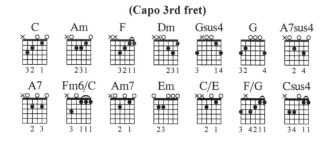

Verse 1

C   Am
If I never knew you,

C   Am
If I never felt this love,

F   Dm
I would have no inkling

F   Gsus4 G
Of how precious life can be.

Verse 2

C   Am
If I never held you,

C   A7sus4 A7
I would never have a   clue

Dm   Fm6/C
How, at last, I'd find in you,

Am   Am7 F
The missing part of me.

Chorus

Dm   Gsus4 G
In this world so full of fear,

Dm   Gsus4 G
Full of rage and lies,

Em   Am
I can see the truth so clear

F   Gsus4
In your eyes, so dry your eyes.

Verse 3

C   Am
And I'm so grateful to you.

C   C/E F
I'd have lived my whole life through,

Dm Em F
Lost for - ever

 Gsus4 G
If I never knew you.

Bridge

F
I thought our love would be so beautiful.

C/E
Somehow we'd make the whole world bright.

Am   Em
I never knew that fear and hate could be so strong,

     Am   Em   F
All they'd leave us were these whispers in the night,

   Dm   Em   F Gsus4
But still my heart is saying we were right.

Verse 4

     C   **Am**
For if I never knew you,

C   **Am**
If I never knew this love,

F   **Dm**
I would have no inkling

        F   **Gsus4**
Of how precious life can be.

Interlude

| **F/G** | | |
| **F** | **C/E** | **Dm**   **Gsus4** |

Verse 5

     C   **Am**
And I'm so grateful to you,

C   **C/E**   **F**
I'd have lived my whole life through,

Dm **Em** **F**
Empty as the sky,

Dm **Em**   **F**
Never knowing why,

Dm   **Em**
Lost for - ever

F **Gsus4** **G**   **C**   **Am**
If I never   knew you.

| **C**   **Csus4** | **C** | |

It's a Small World

from Disney Parks' "it's a small world" attraction

Words and Music by
Richard M. Sherman and Robert B. Sherman

Melody:

It's a world of laugh - ter.

G   D7   C   Am

32   4   213   32 1   231

Verse 1

      G   D7
It's a world of laughter, a world of tears.

                      G
It's a world of hopes and a world of fears.

There's so much that we share
          C   Am
That it's time we're a - ware.
       D7   G
It's a small world after all.

Chorus 1

                 D7
It's a small world after all.
                 G
It's a small world after all.
              C   Am
It's a small world after all.
     D7   G
It's a small, small world.

Verse 2

                       D7
There is just one moon and one golden sun,
                     G
And a smile means friendship to ev'ryone.
                        C   Am
Though the mountains divide and the oceans are wide,
     D7   G
It's a small world after all.

Chorus 2

Repeat Chorus 1

Kiss the Girl
from THE LITTLE MERMAID

Music by Alan Menken
Lyrics by Howard Ashman

Melody:

There you see___ her ___

(Capo 5th fret)

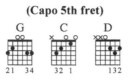

G   C   D

Verse 1

  G
 There you see her,

Sitting there across the way.

C   **G**
She don't got a lot to say, but there's something a - bout her.

     D   **C**
And you don't know why, but you're dying to try.

     G
You wanna kiss the girl.

Verse 2

 G
 Yes, you want her.

Look at her; you know you do.

C   **G**
Possible she wants you, too. There's one way to ask her.

    D   **C**
It don't take a word, not a single word.

     G
Go on and kiss the girl.

Chorus 1

G   C
Sha la la la la la, my, oh, my.

      G
Look at the boy, too shy.

        D   G
Ain't gonna   kiss the girl.

        C
Sha la la la la la, ain't that sad.

      D
Ain't it a shame, too bad.

      G
He gonna   miss the girl.

Verse 3

G
Now's your moment,

Floating in a blue lagoon.

C
Boy, you better do it soon;

      G
Time will be better.

      D   C
She don't say a word and she won't say a word

      G
Until you   kiss the girl.

Chorus 2

G   C
Sha la la la la la, don't be scared.

      G
You got the mood prepared;

      D   G
Go on and   kiss the girl.

        C
Sha la la la la la, don't stop now.

      D
Don't try to hide it how

      G
You wanna   kiss the girl.

Outro-Chorus

           G   C
            Sha la la la la la, float along

           G
And listen   to the song;

                D   G
The song says,   "Kiss the girl."

               C
Sha la la la la la, music play.

             D
Do what the music say.

         G
You gotta   kiss the girl.

Kiss the girl.

Kiss the girl.

Kiss the girl.

Go on and   kiss the girl.

Lava
from LAVA

Music and Lyrics by
James Ford Murphy

Melody:

A long, long   time   a - go

C   G7   F

32 1   32 1   3211

Intro

| C | | | G7 | | | |
| F | | | C | | G7 | | ‖ |

Verse 1

C   G7   F
A long, long time ago   there was a volcano

C   G7
Living all alone in the middle of the sea.

C   G7   F
He sat high above his bay, watching all the couples play,

C   G7   C
And wishing that he had someone too.

G7
And from his lava came this song of hope

F   C   G7
That he sang out loud ev'ry day for years and years.

Chorus 1

F   C
"I have a dream I hope will come true,

G7   C
That you're here with me, and I'm here with you.

F   C
I wish that the earth, sea, and the sky up above-a

F   G7   C
Will send me someone to lava."

Interlude 1

| F | | | G7 | |
| | | C | | | ‖ |

Verse 2

      C   G7
Years of singing all alone turned his lava into stone,

        F   C   G7   C
Un - til   he was on the brink of extinct - tion.

                           G7
But little did he know that, living in the sea below,

        F   C   G7   C
An - other volcano was listening to his song.

                      G7
Ev'ry day she heard his tune, her lava grew and grew,

        F   C   G7   C
Be - cause she believed his song was meant for her.

                     G7
Now she was so ready to meet him above the sea,

        F   C   G7
As he sang his song of hope for the last time.

Chorus 2   *Repeat Chorus 1*

Interlude 2 | C | ||

Verse 3

      C   G7   F
Rising from the sea below stood a lovely volcano,

                     C   G7
Looking all around, but she could not see him.

      C   G7
He tried to sing to let her know that she was not there alone,

        F   C   G7
But with no lava, his song was all gone.

      C
He filled the sea with his tears,

      G7
And watched his dreams disappear

        F   C   G7
As she remembered what his song meant to her.

Chorus 3   *Repeat Chorus 1*

Interlude 3   ‖ C | | | ‖

Verse 4

C   G7   F
Oh, they were so happy to fin'lly meet above the sea.

                    C   G7
All together now their lava grew and grew.

        C
No longer are they all alone

        G7   F
With a - loha as their new home,

                        C   G7
And when you visit them this is what they sing.

Outro-Chorus

F   C
    "I have a dream I hope will come true,

        G7   C
That you'll grow old with me and I'll grow old with you.

F   C
We thank the earth, sea, and the sky we thank too,

    F G7   C
"I   lava   you."

    F G7   C
"I   lava   you."

    F G7   C
"I   lava   you."

Lavender Blue

(Dilly Dilly)

from SO DEAR TO MY HEART

Words by Larry Morey
Music by Eliot Daniel

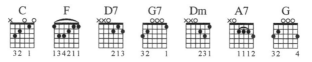

Verse 1

C   F   C
Lavender's blue, dilly, dilly,   lavender's green;

F   C   D7   G7
If I were king, dilly, dilly, I'd need a queen.

Verse 2

C   F   C
Who told me so, dilly, dilly,   who told me so?

F   C   Dm G7   C
I told my - self, dilly, dilly, I   told me so.

Bridge

                   F
If your dilly, dilly heart feels a dilly, dilly way

            A7
'N' if you'll answer, "Yes,"

            G
In the pretty little church on the dilly, dilly day

D7   G7
You'll be wed in the dilly, dilly dress of…

Verse 3

C   F   C
Lavender blue, dilly, dilly,   lavender green,

F   C   Dm   G7   C
Then I'll be king, dilly, dilly and you'll be my queen.

Mickey Mouse March
from THE MICKEY MOUSE CLUB

Words and Music by
Jimmie Dodd

Melody:

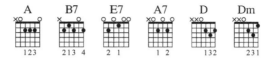

Verse 1

A   B7   E7
Who's the leader of the club that's made for you and me?

A   A7   D   Dm   A   E7   A
M - I - C - K - E - Y   M - O - U - S - E!

Verse 2

A   B7   E7
Hey, there! Hi, there! Ho, there! You're as welcome as can be!

A   A7   D   Dm   A   E7   A
M - I - C - K - E - Y   M - O - U - S - E!

Bridge

       D
Mickey Mouse! (Donald Duck!)

       A
Mickey Mouse! (Donald Duck!)

   B7   E7
For - ever let us hold our banner high!

(High! High! High!)

Verse 3

A   B7   E7
Come along and sing a song and join the jambo - ree!

A   A7   D   Dm   A   E7   A
M - I - C - K - E - Y   M - O - U - S - E!

Let It Go
from FROZEN

Music and Lyrics by
Kristen Anderson-Lopez
and Robert Lopez

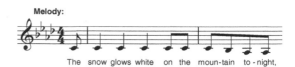

(Capo 1st fret)

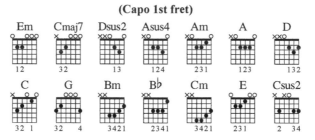

Intro

| Em | Cmaj7 | Dsus2 | Asus4 Am | |
| Em | Cmaj7 | Dsus2 | Asus4 A |

Verse 1

      Em   **Cmaj7**
The snow glows white on the mountain tonight;

  Dsus2   **Asus4 Am**
Not a footprint to be seen.

  Em   **Cmaj7**
A kingdom of iso - lation,

   Dsus2   **Asus4 A Em**
And it looks like I'm the queen.

    Cmaj7
The wind is howling

   Dsus2   **Asus4 Am Em**
Like this swirling storm inside.

     Dsus2   **Asus4**   **A**
Couldn't keep it in, heaven knows I tried.

Pre-Chorus 1

        D   C
Don't let them in, don't let them see;

                                 D
Be the good girl you always have to be.

                          C
Conceal, don't feel, don't let them know...

Well, now they know.

Chorus 1

N.C. G   D
Let it go, let it go,

       Em   C
Can't hold it back any - more.

     G   D
Let it go, let it go,

       Em   C
Turn a - way and slam the door.

G   D   Em   C
I don't care what they're going to say.

       Bm   Bb
Let the storm rage on,

       C   G   D
The cold never bothered me anyway.

Verse 2

Em   C
  It's funny how some dis - tance

       D   Am
Makes ev'rything seem small,

       Em   D
And the fears that once controlled me

       Asus4   A
Can't get to me at all.

Pre-Chorus 2

D   C
   It's time to see what I can do,

                           D
To test the limits and break through.

                                   C
No right, no wrong, no rules for me,

I'm free!

Chorus 2

N.C. G   D
Let it go, let it go,

     Em   C
I am one with the wind and sky.

    G   D
Let it go, let it go,

      Em   C
You'll never see me cry.

G   D   Em   C
Here I stand, and here I'll stay,

     Bm   B♭
Let the storm rage on.

Interlude | C | | | ||

Bridge

C
My power flurries through the air into the ground.

                                                         D
My soul is spiraling in frozen fractals all around.

                                  E
And one thought crystallizes like an icy blast;

         C   D   Am   C
I'm never going back. The past is in the past!

Chorus 3

N.C. G   D
Let it go, let it go,

         Em   C
And I'll rise like the break of dawn.

        G   D
Let it go, let it go,

        Em   C
That perfect girl is gone.

G   D   Em   C   Cm
Here I stand in the light of day,

        Bm   B♭
Let the storm rage on.

        Csus2
The cold never bothered me anyway.

Once Upon a Dream

from SLEEPING BEAUTY

Words and Music by
Sammy Fain and Jack Lawrence
Adapted from a theme by Tchaikovsky

(Capo 5th fret)

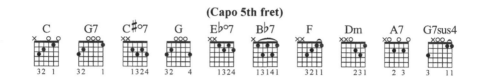

Verse

      C
I know you!

         G7   **C♯°7 G7**
I walked with you once up - on a dream.

G E♭°7 B♭7
I know you!

     G7   **C**
The gleam in your eyes

   F **C G7**
Is so fa - miliar a gleam.

       C
Yet, I know it's true

         Dm   **A7**   **Dm**
That visions are seldom all they seem.

E♭°7 **C**   **A7**
But if I know you,

 Dm   **E♭°7**
I know what you'll do;

       C   **C♯°7**   **A7**
You'll love me at once the way you did

Dm   **G7sus4 G7** **C**
Once up - on a dream.

That's How You Know
from ENCHANTED

Music by Alan Menken
Lyrics by Stephen Schwartz

Melody:

How does she   know _____   you

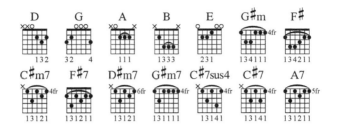

Intro

N.C.
How does she know you love her?

How does she know she's yours?

Refrain 1

N.C.
(How does she know that you love her?)

How do you show her you love her?

How does she know that you really, really, truly love her?

Refrain 2

N.C.
How does she know that you love her?

How do you show her you love her?

How does she know that you really, really, truly love her?

Verse 1

```
D              G           A      D       G  A
It's not enough to take the one you love for granted.

D              G           A      B          E
You must remind her, or she'll be in - clined to say:
```

Chorus 1

```
      A   D    G
"How do I know

A   D        G
He loves me?

      A    D     G
How do I know

A    B      G♯m
He's mine?"
```

Bridge 1

```
         E   F♯  B
Well, does he   leave a little note

      E            C♯m7      F♯7
To tell you you are on his mind?

B                  E          C♯m7      F♯7
Send you yellow flowers when the sky is gray? Hey! _____

D♯m7                G♯m 7    C♯7sus4    C♯7
He'll find a new way to show you a little bit ev'ry day.

F♯7
That's how  you know,

A7                 N.C.
That's how you know he's your love.
```

Interlude 1

```
‖: D      G  |     A   :‖ Play 3 times
 | B      E  |     G  A  |
```

Refrain 3

```
D            G         A        D
  (You've got to show her you need her,

         G        A        D
Don't treat her like a mind - read - er!

       G         A
Each day do something to lead her

B      E     G    A
To be - lieve you love   her.)
```

Verse 2

```
D          G        A   D      G   A
Ev'rybody wants to live happily ever after.

D          G          A    B      E
Ev'rybody wants to know their true love is true.
```

Chorus 2

```
    G A D     G
How do you know

A D         G
He loves you?

   A    D    G
How do you know

A    B    G♯m
He's yours?
```

Bridge 2

```
      E   F♯  B
Well, does he  take you out dancing

E           C♯m7        F♯7
Just so he can hold you close?

B                 E               C♯m7    F♯7
Dedicate a song with words meant just for you? Ooh! ___

D♯m7                G♯m7 C♯7sus4              C♯7
He'll find his own way to tell you  with the little things he'll do.

F♯7
That's  how you know,

A7                N.C.
That's how you know he's your love.
```

Interlude 2

```
|D     G |     A  |D     G |
A      |D     G |     A  |
He's  your   love.

|B     E |
```

Chorus 3

     G A D   G
That's how you know

A D   G
He loves you.

     A   D   G
That's how you know

A B   G#m
It's true.

Bridge 3

     E   F# B
Be - cause he'll wear your fav'rite color

E   C#m7   F#7
Just so he can match your eyes.

B   E   C#m7 F#7
Plan a private picnic by the fire's glow, oh. ____

D#m7   G#m7 C#7sus4   C#7
His heart'll be yours for - ever,   something ev'ry day will show.

F#7
That's how you know,

A7
That's how you know,

F#7
That's how you know,

A7
That's how you know.

F#7
That's how you know,

A7   N.C.   D
That's how you know   he's your love.

Outro-Refrain

                   G   A   D
(That's how she knows that you love her.

                   G   A   D
That's how you show her   you love her.)
                             That's how you know.

                   G   A   D
(You've got to show her you need her.

                   G   A   D
Don't treat her like a mind reader.)
                             That's how you know.

                   G   A   D
(How do you know that you love her?

                   G   A   D
That's how you know that you love her.)
                          He's   your   love.

                   G   A   D
(It's not e - nough to take the one you love for granted!)

Part of Your World
from THE LITTLE MERMAID

Music by Alan Menken
Lyrics by Howard Ashman

Melody:

Look at this stuff. _   Is - n't it neat? _

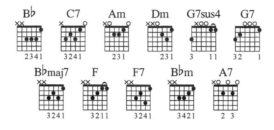

Verse 1

    B♭   **C7**
Look at this stuff. Isn't it neat?

    B♭   **C7**
Wouldn't you think my col - lection's complete?

    Am   **Dm**
Wouldn't you think I'm the girl,

            G7sus4   **G7**
The girl who has ev'rything.

    B♭   **C7**
Look at this trove, treasures untold.

    B♭   **C7**
How many wonders can one cavern hold?

    Am   **Dm**
Looking around here you'd think

            G7sus4   **G7**
Sure, she's got ev'rything.

Pre-Chorus

Bbmaj7   Am
I've got gadgets and gizmos a - plenty.

          Dm   G7sus4   G7
I've got who-zits and what-zits ga - lore.

          Bbmaj7   Am
You want thing-a-ma-bobs, I've got twenty.

          Dm   G7sus4   G7
But who cares? No big deal.

          C7
I want more.

          F   Am
Chorus 1   I wanna be where the people are.

Bb   C7
I wanna see, wanna see 'em dancin',

Dm   Am   C7
Walkin' around on those, what-d'-ya call 'em, oh feet.

F   Am
Flippin' your fins, you don't get too far.

Bb   C7
Legs are required for jumpin', dancin'.

Dm   Am   C7
Strollin' along down the,   what's the word again,   street.

          F   F7
Up where they walk, up where they run,

          Bb   Bbm
Up where they stay all day in the sun.

          F   C7   F
Wanderin' free, wish I could be part of that world.

Bridge

        Bb   C7   Am   Dm
What would I give if I could live outta these waters.

        Bb   C7   Am   F7
What would I pay to spend a day warm on the sand?

      Bb   C7
Betcha on land they under - stand.

      A7   Dm
Bet they don't reprimand their daugh - ters.

      G7sus4   G7
Bright young women, sick of swimmin',

    C7
Ready to stand.

Chorus 2

    F   Am
And ready to know what the people know.

Bb   C7
Ask 'em my questions and get some answers.

Dm   Am   C7
What's a fire, and why does it, what's the word,   burn?

      F
When's it my turn?

      F7   Bb   Bbm
Wouldn't I love, love to ex - plore that shore up a - bove,

N.C.   F
Out of the sea.

      C7   Bb   C7 Bb   C7 F
Wish I could be part of that world.

The Place Where Lost Things Go

from MARY POPPINS RETURNS

Music by Marc Shaiman
Lyrics by Scott Wittman and Marc Shaiman

Melody:

Do you ev-er lie   a - wake at night,

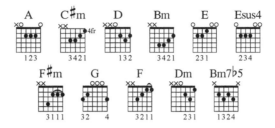

Verse 1

A   C#m D   A
Do you ever lie a - wake at night,

Bm   E
Just between the dark and the morning light,

A   C#m   D   A
Searching for the things you used to know,

Bm   Esus4 E   A
Looking for the place where the lost   things go?

Verse 2

A   C#m   D   A
Do you ever dream or remi - nisce,

Bm   E
Wond'ring where to find what you truly miss?

A   C#m   D   A
Well, maybe all those things that you love so

Bm   Esus4 E   A
Are waiting in the place where the lost   things go.

Bridge 1

C#m   D   C#m   D
Memories you've shared, gone for good, you feared.

     Bm   F#m   G   E
They're all around you still, though they've   disap - peared.

C#m   D   C#m   F
Nothing's really left, or lost without a trace.

Dm   Esus4   E
Nothing's gone forever, only out of   place.

Verse 3

     A   C#m   D   A
So maybe now the dish and my best spoon

  Bm   E
Are playing hide and seek just be - hind the moon,

A   C#m   D   F
Waiting there un - til it's   time to show.

Dm   G   A   Bm7♭5
Spring is like that now, far beneath the snow,

A   F#m   Bm   Esus4   E
Hiding in the place where the lost   things   go.

Interlude |A   C#m |D   A |Bm |Esus4 E   A | ‖

Bridge 2

C#m   D   C#m   D
Time to close your eyes so sleep can come a - round,

   Bm   F#m   G   E
For when you dream, you'll find all that's lost is found.

C#m   D   C#m   F
Maybe on the moon, or maybe somewhere new,

Dm   Esus4 E
Maybe all you're missing lives in - side of you.

Verse 4

       A   C#m   D   A
So, when you need her touch and loving gaze,

 Bm   E
"Gone, but not forgotten," is the perfect phrase.

A   C#m   D   F
Smiling from a star that she makes glow,

Dm   G   A   Bm7♭5
Trust she's always there, watching as you grow.

A   F#m
Find her in the place

               Bm Esus4 E F   B♭ Dm A
Where the lost   things   go.

Reflection
from MULAN

Music by Matthew Wilder
Lyrics by David Zippel

(Capo 2nd fret)

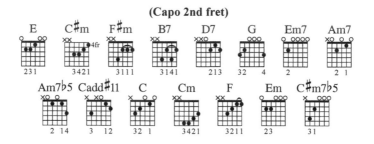

Verse 1

    E   **C#m**
Look at me, I will never pass

    F#m   **B7**
For a perfect bride or a perfect daughter.

E   **C#m**   **D7**
Can it be I'm not meant to play this part?

G   **Em7**   **Am7**
Now I see that if I were truly to be myself,

Am7♭5   **G**
I would break my fam'ly's heart.

Chorus

```
    G         Em7
Who is that girl I see

Cadd#11  C       Cm
Staring      straight back at me?

    G    Em7   C
Why is my re - flection someone

    F      D7
I don't know?

    G         Em7         Cadd#11
Somehow I cannot hide

        C   Cm
Who I am, though I've tried.

    G      Em7   C
When will my re - flection show

Cm          Em   Em7     C#m7b5
Who I am in - side?

    G         Em7   Am7
When will my re - flection show

Cm          G       Em      G
Who I am in - side?
```

Remember Me
(Ernesto de la Cruz)
from COCO

Words and Music by
Kristen Anderson-Lopez and Robert Lopez

Melody:

Re - mem - ber   me,

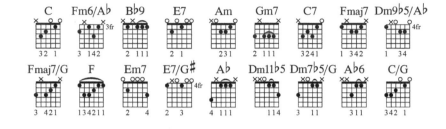

Verse 1

          C
Remember me,

     Fm6/A♭
Though I have to say goodbye.

          C
Remember me,

    B♭9   **E7**
Don't let it make you cry.

     Am
For even if I'm far away,

   Gm7   **C7**
I hold you in my heart.

    Fmaj7
I sing a secret song to you

    Dm9♭5/A♭   **Fmaj7/G**
Each night we are a - part.

Verse 2

            C
Remember me,

      Fm6/A♭
Though I have to travel far.

           C
Remember me,

         Gm7   **C7**
Each time you hear a sad gui - tar.

F
Know that I'm with you

      Em7   **E7/G♯** **Am** **A♭**
The only way that I can   be.

    Dm11♭5
Un - til you're in my arms again,

Dm7♭5/G **A♭**   **A♭6** **C/G**
Re   -   mem - ber   me.

The Siamese Cat Song

from LADY AND THE TRAMP

Words and Music by
Sonny Burke and Peggy Lee

We are Si - am - ee - iz if you plee - iz.

(Capo 1st fret)

Verse 1

    A
We are Siamese if you please.

          E7
We are Siamese if you don't please.

Now we looking over our new domicile.

          A
If we like, we stay for maybe quite a while.

Verse 2

    A
Do you seeing that thing swimming 'round and 'round?

          E7
Maybe we could reaching in and make it drown.

If we sneaking up upon it carefully,

          A
There will be a head for you, a tail for me.

Verse 3

    A
Do you hear what I hear, a baby cry?

          E7
Where we finding baby, there are milk nearby.

If we look in baby buggy, there could be

          A
Plenty milk for you and also some for me.

Some Day My Prince Will Come

from SNOW WHITE AND THE SEVEN DWARFS

Words by Larry Morey
Music by Frank Churchill

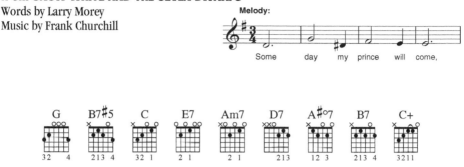

G   B7#5   C   E7
Some - day my prince will come,

Am7   D7
Someday we'll meet again

      G   A#°7   Am7   D7
And a - way to his castle we'll go.

      G   A#°7   Am7   D7
I'll be happy for - ever, I know.

G   B7#5   C   E7
Some - day when spring is here,

Am7   D7
We'll find our love a-new

      G   B7
And the birds will sing

      C+   A#°7
And wedding bells will ring

      G   Am7   D7   G
Some - day when my dreams come true.

A Spoonful of Sugar

from MARY POPPINS

Words and Music by
Richard M. Sherman and Robert B. Sherman

(Capo 1st fret)

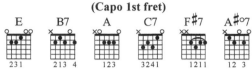

Verse 1

          E
In ev'ry job that must be done

There is an element of fun.

                                B7
You find the fun and snap the job's a game.

             A   **C7**
And ev'ry task you under - take

      E   **F#7**
Be - comes a piece of cake,

    E   **B7**
A lark! A spree!

                    A#°7
It's very clear to see that a…

Chorus 1

B7   **E**
Spoonful of sugar helps the medicine go down,

   B7   **E**
The medicine go down, medicine go down.

A#°7 **B7**   **E**
Just a spoonful of sugar helps the medicine go down

                    B7   **E**
In a most de - lightful way.

Verse 2

                  E
A robin feathering his nest

Has very little time to rest

                            B7
While gathering his bits of twine and twig.

            A   C7
Though quite in - tent in his pur - suit

  E   F$\sharp$7
He has a merry tune to toot.

  E   B7
He knows a song will move the job along.
A$\sharp$°7
For a...

Chorus 2   *Repeat Chorus 1*

Verse 3

              E
The honey - bees that fetch the nectar

From the flowers to the comb

                        B7
Never tire from ever buzzing to and fro

        A   C7
Because they take a little nip

        E   F$\sharp$7
From every flower that they sip

   E
And hence (And hence)

   B7
They find (They find)

Their task is not a grind
A$\sharp$°7
When a...

Chorus 3   *Repeat Chorus 1*

Supercalifragilisticexpialidocious

from MARY POPPINS

Words and Music by
Richard M. Sherman
and Robert B. Sherman

Melody:

Su - per - cal - i - frag - il - is - tic - ex - pi - al - i - do - cious!

(Capo 3rd fret)

G	D7	G7	C	A7

Chorus 1

      G   D7
Supercalifragilisticexpiali - docious!

                                 G
Even though the sound of it is something quite a - trocious,

                        G7   C
If you say it loud enough you'll always sound pre - cocious.

             G   D7   G
Supercali - fragilistic - expiali - docious!

Bridge 1

      G   D7
Um, diddle, diddle, diddle, um, diddle, ay!

      G   D7
Um, diddle, diddle, diddle, um, diddle, ay!

      G   D7
Um, diddle, diddle, diddle, um, diddle, ay!

      G   D7
Um, diddle, diddle, diddle, um, diddle, ay!

Verse 1

        G   D7
Be - cause I was afraid to speak when I was just a lad,

                                 G
Me father gave me nose a tweak and told me I was bad.

                                        C
But then one day I learned a word that saved me achin' nose,

      A7   D7
The biggest word you ever 'eard and this is 'ow it goes! Oh!

Chorus 2	*Repeat Chorus 1*
Bridge 2	*Repeat Bridge 1*

Verse 2

G   D7
He traveled all around the world, and ev'rywhere he went,

                                        G
He'd use his word and all would say, "There goes a clever gent."

                                  C
When dukes and maharajahs pass the time 'o day with me,

A7   D7
I say me special word and then they ask me out to tea! Oh!

Chorus 3	*Repeat Chorus 1*
Bridge 3	*Repeat Bridge 1*

Verse 3

G   D7
So when the cat has got your tongue, there's no need for dis - may,

                                        G
Just summon up this word and then you've got a lot to say.

                              G7   C
But better use it carefully or it could change your life.

          A7   D7
One night I said it to my girl and now me girl's me wife!

Chorus 4

          G   D7
She's supercalifragilisticexpiali - docious!

                               G
Supercalifragilisticexpiali - docious!

                        G7   C
Supercalifragilistic - expiali - docious!

                 G   D7   G
Supercali - fragilistic - expiali - docious!

Outro |C |G |D7 |G   ‖

Under the Sea
from THE LITTLE MERMAID

Music by Alan Menken
Lyrics by Howard Ashman

The sea - weed is al - ways green - er

(Capo 3rd fret)

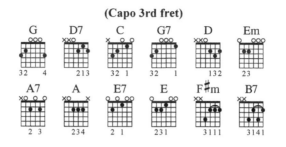

Intro

‖: G | D7 G | | D7 G :‖

Verse 1

    G   D7   G
The seaweed is always greener

          D7   G
In somebody else's lake.

          D7   G
You dream about going up there,

          D7   G   C
But that is a big mis - take.

              G   D7
Just look at the world around you,

             G   C
Right here on the ocean floor.

             G   D7
Such wonderful things surround you.

             G
What more is you lookin' for?

Chorus 1

N.C. C G   D7 G
Under the sea, under the sea.

      C   D7
Darlin', it's better down where it's wetter,

     G G7
Take it from me.

      C   D
Up on the shore, they work all day.

      Em   A7
Out in the sun, they slave away

       C   D7
While we de - votin' full time to floatin'

      G D7 G   D7 G
Under the sea.

Verse 2

G   D7 G
 Down here, all the fish is happy

       D7   G
As off through the waves they roll.

      D7   G
The fish on the land ain't happy.

        D7 G C
They sad 'cause they in the bowl.

      G   D7
But fish in the bowl is lucky,

      G   C
They in for a worser fate.

        G   D7
One day when the boss gets hungry,

       G
Guess who gon' be on the plate?

Chorus 2

N.C.   C   G   **D7**   G
Under the sea,   under the sea,

      C   **D7**   **G**   **G7**
Nobody beat us, fry us and eat us in fricas - see.

           C   **D**
We what the land folks loves to cook.

         Em   **A7**
Under the sea, we off the hook.

        C   **D7**
We got no troubles, life is the bubbles

Chorus 3

         C   **G**   **D7**   **G**
Under the sea,   under the sea.

      C   **D7**   **G**   **G7**
Since life is sweet here, we got the beat here, natural - ly.

      C   **D**   **Em**   **A7**
Even the sturgeon an' the ray, they get the urge 'n start to play.

       C   **D7**   **G**   **D7**   **G**
We got the spirit, you got to hear it, under the sea.

Bridge

     D7   **G**
The newt play the flute. The carp play the harp.

     D7   **G**
The plaice play the bass. And they soundin' sharp.

     C   **G**
The bass play the brass. The chub play the tub.

     D7   **G**
The fluke is the duke of soul.

     D7   **G**
The ray, he can play. The ling's on the strings.

     D7   **G**
The trout rockin' out. The blackfish, she sings.

     C   **G**
The smelt and the sprat, they know where it's at.

     D7   **G**
An' oh, that blowfish blow.

Interlude

C	G	D7	G	
C	D7	G	G7	
C	D	Em	A7	
C	D7			
G	D7 G		D7 G	
A	E7 A			

Chorus 4

      D   **A**   **E7**   **A**
Under the sea,   under the sea.

         D   **E7**   **A** **A7**
When the sar - dine begin the be - guine, it's music to me.

        D   **E**
What do they got, a lot of sand.

    F♯m   **B7**
We got a hot crustacean band.

        D   **E7**   **A**   **E7**
Each little clam here know how to jam here under the sea.

A   **D**   **E7**   **A**   **E7**
Each little slug here cuttin' a rug here under the sea.

A   **D**   **E**
Each little snail here know how to wail here.

      F♯m   **B7**
That's why it's hotter under the water.

        D   **E7**
Yeah, we in luck here down in the muck here

      A   **E7 A**   **E7 A**
Under the sea.

Westward Ho, the Wagons!

from WESTWARD HO, THE WAGONS!

Words by Tom Blackburn
Music by George Bruns

Melody:

West-ward   roll   the   wa-gons,

C   F   G7   C7   Fm

32 1   3211   32 1   3241   3111

Intro

N.C.   C
Foreward, ho!

Chorus 1

               C   F   C
Westward roll the wagons, always westward roll.

                                   G7   C
Westward roll the wagons, for Oregon's our goal.

Verse 1

             C   C7   F
There's magic in the wind and a brightness in the sky.

                          C   G7 C
There's a promise land a - waitin' and we'll get there bye and bye.

Chorus 2

Repeat Chorus 1

Verse 2

             C   C7   F
A - merica's in mo - tion and their hopes are turnin' west.

                     C   G7 C
Hey, let's all get it goin', for a new land's always best.

Chorus 3

Repeat Chorus 1

Verse 3	C C7 F Keep the bullwhips crackin' and a smile on ev'ry face.

                                C   G7   C
Keep the teams all pullin' and each wagon in its place.

Chorus 4   *Repeat Chorus 1*

Verse 4
C   C7   F
Where the ruts all deeper a - long the Oregon Trail.

                                C   G7   C
There's a thousand wagons bound to follow in our trail.

Chorus 5   *Repeat Chorus 1*

Verse 5
               C   C7   F
There's magic in the wind and a brightness in the sky.

                                  C   G7   C
Hey, there's a promised land a - waitin' and we'll get there bye and bye.

Chorus 6   *Repeat Chorus 1*

Outro
                   F   Fm
Westward roll, westward roll,

                 C
Westward roll.   *Roll!*

A Whale of a Tale

from 20,000 LEAGUES UNDER THE SEA

Words and Music by
Norman Gimbel and Al Hoffman

Melody:

Got a whale of a tale to tell ya.

(Capo 1st fret)

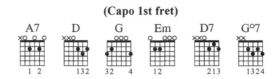

A7   D   G   Em   D7   G°7

Chorus 1

```
     A7   D              G    A7
Got a whale of a tale to tell ya, lads,

     D              Em   A7
A whale of a tale or two

         D    D7      G      A7
'Bout the flappin' fish and the girls I've loved,

     D       A7        D       A7
On nights like this with the moon a - bove.

     D       A7     D    G°7
A whale of a tale and it's all true,

     D       A7     D    G    D
I swear by my tat - too.
```

Verse 1

          G   D
There was Mermaid Minnie,

                          D7
Met her down in Mada - gascar,

G   D
She would kiss me

                  D7
Anytime that I would ask her.

G   D   A7
Then one evening her flame of love blew out.

D   A7   D
Blow me down and pick me up!

        Em   A7 D
She swapped me for a trout.

Chorus 2   *Repeat Chorus 1*

Verse 2

          G   D
There was Typhoon Tessie,

                      D7
Met her on the coast of Java,

G   D
When we kissed I

                  D7
Bubbled up like molten lava.

G   D   A7
Then she gave me the scare of my young life.

D   A7 D
Blow me down and pick me up!

        Em   A7   D
She was the captain's wife.

Chorus 3   *Repeat Chorus 1*

Interlude

D	A7	D	
	A7	D	

                            G   D
Verse 3   There was Harpoon Hannah,

                                        D7
                         Had a face that made you shudder,

                         G   D
                         Lips like fish hooks,

                                        D7
                         And a nose just like a rudder.

                         G   D   A7
                         If I kissed her, and held her tender - ly

                         (Held her tenderly…)

                               D   A7 D   Em A7   D
                         There's no sea mon - ster big enough to ever frighten me.

                         A7 D   G   A7
Chorus 4   Got a whale of a tale to tell ya, lads,

                            D   Em   A7
                         A whale of a tale or two

                               D   D7   G   A7
                         'Bout the flappin' fish and the girls I've loved,

                            D   A7   D   A7
                         On nights like this with the moon a - bove.

                            D   A7   D
                         A whale of a tale and it's all true,

                          Em   A7   D
                         I swear by my tat - too!

When She Loved Me
from TOY STORY 2

Music and Lyrics by
Randy Newman

Melody:

When some - bod - y loved me,

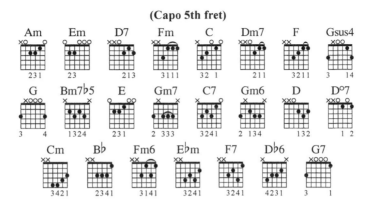

(Capo 5th fret)

Intro |Am Em |D7 Fm |C | ||

Verse 1

     C   Dm7 C
When some - body loved me,

     F   D7   Gsus4   G
Ev'ry - thing was beautiful.

     Bm7♭5 E   Am   C
Ev'ry   hour we spent togeth - er

     F   G
Lives within my heart.

Verse 2

     C   Dm7 C
And when she was sad,

     F   D7   Gsus4 G
I was there to dry her tears.

     Bm7♭5 E   Am
And when she was happy,

     C   F   C G7 C
So was I when she loved me.

Bridge 1

F
Through the summer and the fall,

    C   Gm7 C7   F
We had each other, that was all.

    C   F   C   D7
Just she and I to - gether,

               G7
Like it was meant to be.

Verse 3

C   Dm7   C
And when she was lonely,

F   D7   Gsus4 G
I was there to comfort her,

    C7 F   C G7 C
And I knew that she loved me.

Bridge 2

Am   Gm6   C
So the years went by, I stayed the same.

    D   D°7   C   Cm
But she be - gan to drift a - way,

Bb   E   Am
I was left a - lone.

Fm6 G   Ebm F7
Still I waited for the day

           Db6   Ebm G7
When she'd say, "I will always love   you."

Verse 4

C   Dm7   C
Lonely and for - gotten,

F   D7   Gsus4 G
Never thought she'd look my way,

Bm7♭5 E   Am   C
And she smiled at me and held me

F   G
Just like she used to do,

C7   F   C G7
Like she loved me when she loved me.

Outro

C   Dm7 C
When some - body loved me,

F   D7   Gsus4   G
Ev'ry - thing was beautiful.

Bm7♭5 E   Am   C
Ev'ry   hour we spent togeth - er

F   G   C G7   C
Lives within my heart, when she loved me.

When You Wish Upon a Star

from PINOCCHIO

Words by Ned Washington
Music by Leigh Harline

Melody:

When you wish up - on a star,

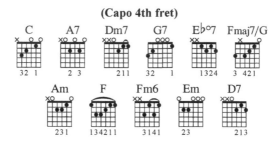

(Capo 4th fret)

Verse 1

     C   A7   Dm7
When you wish up - on a star,

     G7   E♭°7   C
Makes no diff'rence who you are,

       E♭°7   Dm7   Fmaj7/G
Any - thing your heart de - sires

       Dm7 G7 C   G7
Will come to   you.

Verse 2

C   A7   Dm7
If your heart is in your dream,

G7   Eb°7   C
No request is too ex - treme,

             Eb°7   Dm7 Fmaj7/G
When you wish up - on a star

   Dm7   G7   C
As dream - ers do.

Bridge

Fm6   G7 C   Fm6
Fate is   kind,

         G7 Eb°7   C   Am
She brings to   those who love,

         Eb°7   D7   Fm6 G7
The sweet fulfillment of their secret long - ing.

Verse 3

C   A7   Dm7
Like a bolt out of the blue,

G7   Eb°7   C
Fate steps in and sees you thru,

             Eb°7   Dm7 Fmaj7/G
When you wish up - on a star

   Dm7 G7   C
Your dream comes true.

Whistle While You Work
from SNOW WHITE AND THE SEVEN DWARFS

Words by Larry Morey
Music by Frank Churchill

Melody:

Just whis-tle while you work.

D   D#°7   A7   A°7   A7#5   Em7   G   Gm7

Intro

| D | | D#°7 | A7 A°7 | A7

Verse 1

A7#5   D
Just   whistle while you work *(Whistle)*

   Em7   A7   Em7
And cheerful - ly to - gether

A7   Em7 A7   D   A7
We can tidy   up this place.

Verse 2

   D
So hum a merry tune *(Hum)*

   Em7   A7   Em7   A7
It won't take long when there's a song

   Em7   A7   D
To help you set the pace.

Bridge

   G
And as you sweep the room,

Imagine that the broom

   Gm7
Is someone that you love,

      D   D°7   Em7   A7
And soon you'll find you're dancing to the tune.

Verse 3

| D | | | |

   Em7   A7   Em7   A7
When hearts are high, the time moves on,

   Em7 A7   D
So whistle while you work.

A Whole New World
from ALADDIN

Music by Alan Menken
Lyrics by Tim Rice

(Capo 1st fret)

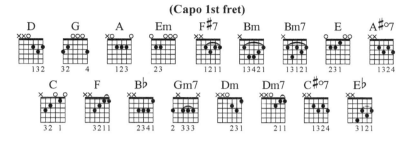

Verse 1

      D
I can show you the world,

              G   **A**
Shining, shimmering, splen - did.

Em   **F#7**
Tell me princess,

        Bm   **Bm7**   **G**   **D**
Now when did you last let your heart de - cide?

Verse 2

      D
I can open your eyes,

              G   **A**
Take you wonder by won - der.

Em **F#7**   **Bm**
Over, sideways and under

Bm7 **G**   **D**
On a magic carpet ride.

Chorus 1

          A   **D**
A whole new world,

         A   **D**
A new fan - tastic point of view.

        G   **D**   **G**   **D**
No one to tell us no or where to go

 Bm   **E**   **A**
Or say we're only dream - ing.

              D
A whole new world,

      A   **A#°7**   **Bm**
A dazzling place I never knew.

D   **G**   **D**   **G**   **D**
But, when I'm way up here, it's crystal clear

  Bm   **E**   **C**   **A**   **D**
That now I'm in a whole new world with you.

Verse 3

F
Unbelievable sights,

        B♭ **C**
Indescribable feel - ing.

Gm7 **A**   **Dm**
Soaring, tumbling, free - wheeling

Dm7   **B♭**   **F**
Through an endless diamond sky.

Chorus 2

        C   F
A whole new world,

          C   F
A hundred thousand things to see.

       Bb   F   Bb   F
I'm like a shooting star, I've come so far,

 Dm   G   Bb
I can't go back to where…

        C   F   Dm
A whole new world

         C   C#°7
With new ho - rizons to pur - sue.

F   Bb   F   Bb   F
I'll chase them any - where, there's time to spare.

Dm   G   Eb   C   Dm   Dm7
Let me share this whole new world with you.

Outro

        Bb
A whole new world,

F   Gm7
That's where we'll be.

F   Bb   C
A thrilling chase. A wond'rous place

       F
For you and me.

Who's Afraid of the Big Bad Wolf?

from THREE LITTLE PIGS

Words and Music by Frank Churchill
Additional Lyric by Ann Ronell

Intro		G		D7				G	D7	

Chorus 1

    G   D7
Who's afraid of the big bad wolf,

           G
Big bad wolf, big bad wolf?

           D7
Who's afraid of the big bad wolf?

       G   D7
Tra, la, la, la, la.

G   D7
Who's afraid of the big bad wolf,

           G
Big bad wolf, big bad wolf?

           D7
Who's afraid of the big bad wolf?

       G
Tra, la, la, la, la.

Verse 1

A7   D   G   D   A7
Long a - go there were three pigs,

       D   G   D
Little handsome piggy wigs.

A7   D
For the big bad, very big,

G   A7   D
Very bad wolf they didn't give three figs.

Verse 2

A7   D   G D   A7
Number one was very gay,

       D   G   D
And he built his house with hay.

A7   D   G
With a hey-hey toot, he blew on his flute,

       A7   D   D7
And he played around all day.

Bridge 1

G   C♯7   F♯m   B7
Number two was fond of jigs,

     Em A7   D   G♯°7 D
And so he built his house with   twigs.

G   C♯7   F♯m   B7
Heigh diddle diddle, he played on his fiddle

     E7   A7
And danced with lady pigs.

Verse 3

       D   G   D   A7
Number three said, "Nix on tricks.

       D   G   D
I will build my house with bricks."

A7 D   G
He   had no chance to sing and dance 'cause

A7   D
Work and play don't mix!

Interlude 1	**N.C.** Ha, ha, ha! The two little, do little pigs
	Just winked and laughed ha, ha!
Chorus 2	*Repeat Chorus 1*

Verse 4

```
A7        D       G      D    A7
Come the day when fate did frown

         D       G  D
And the wolf blew into town.

A7    D                      G
With a gruff "puff, puff" he puffed just enough,

       A7                D
And the hay house fell right down.
```

Verse 5

```
A7      D       G       D    A7
One and two were scared to death

       D     G      D
Of the big bad wolfie's breath.

  A7    D                       G
"By the hair of your chinny-chin I'll blow you in."

        A7                 D    D7
And the twig house answered, "yes."
```

Bridge 2

G   C#7   F#m   B7
No one left but number three

    Em   A7   D   G#°7 D
To save the piglet fam - i - ly.

G   C#7   F#m   B7
When they knocked, he fast un - locked

    E7   A7
And said, "Come in with me!"

Verse 6

    D   G   D   A7
Now they all were safe in - side,

    D   G   D
And the bricks hurt wolfie's pride.

A7   D   G
So he slid down the chimney and, oh, by Jim'ney,

    A7   D
In the fire he was fried.

Interlude 2

N.C.
Ha, ha, ha! The three little, free little pigs

Rejoiced and laughed ha, ha!

Chorus 3

Repeat Chorus 1

Written in the Stars

from AIDA

Music by Elton John
Lyrics by Tim Rice

Melody:

I am here to tell __ you

C	G/C	F/C	Gb	Ab	Bbsus2	E	E7	Am
32 1	3 4	34211	134211	134211 4fr	3411	231	2 1	231

Am/G	F	Gsus4	G	E7sus4	C/E	Dm7	C/G	G/B
4 231	134211	3 14	32 4	2 3	32 1	211	342 1	2 4

Intro

| C   G/C F/C | C   G/C F/C | Gb Ab Bbsus2 |

Verse 1

        C   G/C F/C   C   E   E7
Male: I am here to tell   you we can never meet again.

Am   **Am/G**
Simple really, isn't it?

  F   **Gsus4 G C**   **G/C F/C**
A word or two and then   a lifetime of not know - ing

        C   **E7sus4 E7**
Where or how or why or when

   Am   **Am/G**   **F**   **C/E**
You think of me or speak of me or wonder what befell

   Dm7   **C/G**   **G**
The someone you once loved so long a - go, so well.

                             C   G/C F/C   C   E7sus4 E7
Verse 2   *Female:* Never wonder what   I'll feel as living shuffles by.

                 Am   Am/G   F   Gsus4 G
                 You don't have to ask me and I need not reply.

                 C   G/C F/C   C   E7sus4 E7
                 Ev'ry moment of   my life from now until I die

                 Am   Am/G   F   C/E
                 I will think or dream of you and fail to understand

                     Dm7   C/G   G
                 How a perfect love can be confounded out of hand.

                         C   G/B
Chorus 1   *Both:* Is it written in the stars?

                     Am   Am/G
                 Are we paying for some crime?

                     F   Dm7   C/G
                 Is that all that we are good for, just a stretch of mortal time?

                 G   C   G/B Am   Am/G
                 Is this God's experiment   in   which we have no say?

                    F
                 In which we're given paradise,

                   Dm7 C   G
                 But only   for   a day?

Interlude | C   G/C F/C | C   G/C F/C |

                     C   G/C F/C
Verse 3   *Male:* Nothing can be al - tered.

                        C   E7sus4 E7
                 Oh, there is nothing to decide.

                 Am   Am/G   F   Gsus4 G
                 No escape, no change of heart, nor any place to hide.

                     C   G/C F/C   C   E7sus4 E7
                 Female: You're all I ev - er want but this I am denied.

                 Am   Am/G   F   C/E
                 Sometimes in my darkest thoughts I wish I never learned

                     Dm7   C/G   G
                 Both: What it is to be in love and have that love returned.

Chorus 2

                              C
Both: Is it written in the stars?

G/B   Am   Am/G
Oh, are we paying for some crime?

        F   C/E   Dm7   Gsus4
Is that all that we are good for,   just a stretch of mortal time?

G   C   G/B Am   Am/G
Is this God's experiment, oh, in which we have no say?

   F   C/E Dm7 Gsus4 G
In which we're given paradise, but   only   for a day?

     C   G/B
(Is it written in the stars?)

      Am   Am/G
(Are we paying for some crime?)

        F   C/G   Dm7   Gsus4
(Is that all that we are good for, just a stretch of mortal time?)

      G   C   G/B Am
Both: Is this God's experiment *Male:* in   which we have no say?

                   Am/G
Female: In which we have no say,

        F   C/E
Male: In which we're given paradise *Female:* Given paradise

      Dm7 Gsus4 G
Both: Only   for a day.

Outro |C   G/C F/C |C   G/C F/C |G♭ A♭ B♭sus2 |C   ‖

You'll Be in My Heart (Pop Version)

from TARZAN™

Words and Music by
Phil Collins

Melody:

Come stop your cry - ing; _ it will be all right.

(Capo 1st fret)

F   Bb   Gm   C   A   D   G   F#m7   Bm   A7sus4

3211   2341   3111   32 1   123   132   32   4   2 111   3421   1234

Gsus4   Gsus2   Emb6   Em   Esus4   E   B   G#m7   C#m

3 14   2 1 4   23 1   23   234   231   2341   2 333   3421

Intro | F | | | ||

Verse 1
       F
       Come stop your crying, it will be all right.

                           Bb
       Just take my hand, hold it tight.

                                        Gm
       I will protect you from all around you.

                    C
       I will be here, don't you cry.

Verse 2
       F
       For one so small you seem so strong.

                                        Bb
       My arms will hold you, keep you safe and warm.

                              Gm
       This bond between us can't be broken.

                    C   A
       I will be here, don't you cry.

	D **G**
Chorus 1	'Cause you'll be in my heart,

     A   **F♯m7**
Yes, you'll be in my heart

     Bm   **G**   **C**   **A**
From this day on, now and forever - more.

D   **G**
You'll be in my heart

     A   **F♯m7**
No matter what they say.

     Bm   **G**   **C**   **A7sus4** **G**   **A**
You'll be here in my heart al - ways.

F

Verse 3   Why can't they understand the way we feel?

                                              B♭
They just don't trust what they can't explain.

                                       Gm
I know we're diff'rent, but deep inside us

                      C   **A**
We're not that different at all.

     D   **G**
Chorus 2   And you'll be in my heart,

     A   **F♯m7**
Yes, you'll be in my heart

     Bm   **G**   **C**   **A**
From this day on, now and forever - more.

    Gsus4 G   **Gsus2**   **G**
Don't listen to them, 'cause what do they know?

    Em♭6   **Em**   **Esus4 Em**
We need each other to have, to hold.

    Bm   **C**
They'll see in time,   I know.

    Gsus4 G   **Gsus2**   **G**
When destiny calls you, you must be strong.

  Em♭6   **Em**   **Esus4**   **Em**
It may not be with you, but you've got to hold on.

    Bm   **C**
They'll see in time,   I ___ know.

    D   **A**
We'll show them to - gether,

    E   **A**
'Cause you'll be in my heart.

     B   **G♯m7**
Believe me, you'll be in my heart.

     C♯m   **A**   **D**   **B**
I'll be there from this day on, now and forevermore.

E   **A**
You'll be in my heart, (You'll be here in my heart.)

 B   **G♯m7**
No matter what they say, (I'll be with you.)

   C♯m   **A**   **D**   **B**
You'll be in my heart (I'll be there.) al - ways,

  A   **E**
Al - ways.   I'll be with you.

    A   **E**
I'll be there for you always, always and al - ways.

     A
Just look o - ver your shoulder.

     E
Just look o - ver your shoulder.

     A
Just look o - ver your shoulder,

        E
I'll be there always.

Yo Ho
(A Pirate's Life for Me)
from Disney Parks'
Pirates of the Caribbean attraction

Words by Xavier Atencio
Music by George Bruns

Yo   ho,   yo   ho,   a

F   B♭   C7   Dm   A7   Gm   G7

3211	3331	3241	231	1 2	444	32 1

Chorus 1

        F   B♭ F   C7   F
Yo ho, yo   ho, a pirate's life for me.

Verse 1

         Dm   A7
We pillage, plunder, we rifle and loot.

         Dm   A7
Drink up me 'earties, yo ho.

         Gm   C7   F   Dm
We kidnap and ravage and don't give a hoot.

         G7   C7
Drink up me 'earties, yo ho.

Chorus 2

        F   B♭ F   C7   F
Yo ho, yo   ho, a pirate's life for me.

Verse 2

         Dm   A7
We extort and pilfer, we filch and sack.

         Dm   A7
Drink up me 'earties, yo ho.

         Gm   C7   F   Dm
Ma - raud and Em - bezzle and even hi - jack.

         G7   C7
Drink up me 'earties, yo ho.

Chorus 3	F B♭ F C7 F Yo ho, yo ho, a pirate's life for me.

Verse 3

        Dm   A7
We kindle and char and in - flame and ignite.

        Dm   A7
Drink up me 'earties, yo ho.

       Gm   C7   F   Dm
We burn up the city, we're really a fright.

       G7   C7
Drink up me 'earties, yo ho.

Verse 4

        Dm   A7
We're rascals and scoundrels, we're villains and knaves.

        Dm   A7
Drink up me 'earties, yo ho.

       Gm   C7   F   Dm
We're devils and black sheep, we're really bad eggs.

       G7   C7
Drink up me 'earties, yo ho.

Chorus 4

F   B♭   F   C7   F
Yo ho, yo   ho, a pirate's life for me.

Verse 5

        Dm   A7
We're beggars and blighters and ne'er-do-well cads.

        Dm   A7
Drink up me 'earties, yo ho.

Gm   C7   F   Dm
Aye, but we're loved by our mommies and dads.

       G7   C7
Drink up me 'earties, yo ho.

Outro-Chorus

F   B♭   F   C7   F
Yo ho, yo   ho, a pirate's life for me.

You're Welcome
from MOANA

Music and Lyrics by
Lin-Manuel Miranda

Melody:

I see what's hap - pen - ing, yeah: ___

C   F/C   B♭sus2/C   B♭   B♭/C   Am   E

Verse 1

```
            C                              F/C   Bbsus2/C
      I see what's happening, yeah:

                                          C
      You're face to face with greatness, and it's strange.

                                    F/C      Bbsus2/C
      You don't even know how to feel. It's a - dorable.

                                    C
      Well, it's nice to see that humans never change.

                          F/C
      Open your eyes. Let's begin:

            Bbsus2/C                    C
      Yes it's really me, it's Maui. Breathe it in.

                              F/C
      I know it's a lot: the hair, the bod,

                  Bb        Bb/C
      When you're staring at a demigod.
```

Chorus 1

```
      Am          F/C
        What can I say   except,

                  C           E              Am
      "You're wel - come, for the tides,  the sun, the sky"?

            F/C               C
      Hey, it's okay,  it's okay: you're wel - come.

            E
      I'm just an ordinary demiguy.
```

Verse 2

C   F/C
   Hey, what has two thumbs and pulled up the sky

       B♭sus2/C   C
When you were waddling yea-high? *This guy!*

                      F/C   B♭sus2/C
When the nights got cold, who stole you fire from down below?

You're looking at him, yo.

C   F/C   B♭sus2/C
Oh, also, I lassoed the sun. *You're welcome…*

                            C
To stretch your days and bring you fun.

               B♭/C   F/C
Also, I harnessed the breeze, *You're welcome…*

  B♭   B♭/C
To fill your sails and shake your trees.

Chorus 2

Am   F/C
   So what can I say, except,

           C   E   Am
"You're wel - come, for the is - lands I pulled from the sea?"

               F/C   C
There's no need to pray, it's okay, you're wel - come. *Huh!*

  E   Am
I guess it's just my way of being me!

         F/C   C
You're wel - come! You're wel - come! *Well, come to think of it:*

Rap:

     C   N.C.
Kid, honestly, I could go on and on.

                                       C
I could explain ev'ry nat'ral phenomenon.

N.C.
The tide? The grass? The ground?

Oh, that was Maui, just messing around.

C   N.C.
I killed an eel, I buried it's guts.

Sprouted a tree: now you got coconuts!

C   N.C.
What's the lesson? What is the takeaway?

                                       Am
Don't mess with Maui when he's on a breakaway.

N.C.   F/C
And the tapestry here in my skin

Is a map of the vict'ries I win!

C   N.C.
Look where I've been! I make ev'rything happen!

E
Look at that mean mini Maui,

Just tickety tappin'! Heh, heh, heh,

Heh, heh, heh, hey!

Chorus 3

        Am   F/C
        Well, anyway, let me say,

                C   E   Am
        "You're wel - come, for the won - derful world you know."

            F/C   C
        Hey, it's okay, it's okay: you're wel - come.

            E   Am
        Well, come to think of it, I gotta go.

                F/C   C
        Hey, it's your day to say, "You're wel - come,"

            E   Am
        'Cause I'm gonna need that boat.

                F/C
        I'm sailing away, away.

                C   E
        You're wel - come, 'cause Maui can do ev'rything but float!

Outro

        Am   F/C   C   F/C C N.C.
        You're wel - come! You're wel - come!

                C N.C.
        And thank you.

You've Got a Friend in Me

from TOY STORY

Music and Lyrics by
Randy Newman

Melody:

You got a friend in me.

(Capo 1st fret)

D   F#7   Bm   Bb7   D°7   A7   A7#5   D7   G

G7   E7   B7   Db   D6   Ebm   Bb°7   F#m   Em

Intro

| D   F#7 | Bm   Bb7 | D   D°7   A7 | D   ‖

Verse 1

```
D              A7#5   D7      G
You've got a friend in me.

         D°7        D       G
You've got a friend in me.

          D        F#7      Bm
When the road looks     rough a - head

          G         D              F#7       Bm       G
And you're miles and miles from your nice warm bed,

          D                  G7    Bm
You just re - member what your old pal said,

          E7        A7          D       B7
"Boy, you've got a friend in me.

          E7          A7
Yeah, you've got a friend in me."
```

Interlude

| D   F#7 | Bm   Bb7 | D   D°7   A7 ‖

Verse 2

D   A7#5   D7   G
You've got a friend in me.

             D°7   D   G
You've got a friend in me.

         D   F#7   Bm   G
You got troubles, then I got 'em, too.

           D   F#7   Bm
There isn't anything I wouldn't do for you.

G   D   F#7 Bm
If we stick to - gether we can see it through,

     E7   A7   D B7 E7
'Cause you've got a friend in me.

        A7   D
You've got a friend in me.

Bridge

G   Db   D6
    Now, some other folks might be a little smarter than I am,

           D°7   D6   Db
Bigger and stronger, too.   Maybe.

         Ebm   Bb°7 Db   F#m B7
But none of them will ever love you the way I do,

     Em   A7
Just me and you, boy.

Verse 3

D   A7#5   D7
    And as the years go by,

     G   D°7 D   G
Our friendship will never die.

           D°7   D   Bm   E7
You're gonna see it's our desti - ny.

        A7   D   B7   E7
You've got a friend in me.

        A7   D   B7   E7
You've got a friend in me.

        A7
You've got a friend in me.

Outro |D   F#7 |Bm Bb7 |D   D°7 A7 |D   ‖

Zip-A-Dee-Doo-Dah
from SONG OF THE SOUTH

Music by Allie Wrubel
Words by Ray Gilbert

G   C   A7   D7

Verse 1

     G   C   G
Zip-a-dee-doo-dah, zip-a-dee-ay,

C   G   A7   D7
My, oh my, what a wonderful day!

G   C   G
Plenty of sunshine, headin' my way.

C   G   A7 D7 G
Zip-a-dee-doo - dah, zip-a-dee-ay!

Bridge 1

          D7   G
Mister Bluebird on my shoulder.

       A7   D7
It's the truth, it's "actch'll."

N.C.
Ev'rything is "satisfactch'll."

Verse 2

     G   C   G
Zip-a-dee-doo-dah, zip-a-dee-ay!

C   G   A7   D7 G
Wonderful feeling, wonder - ful day.

Verse 3   *Repeat Verse 1*

Bridge 2   *Repeat Bridge 1*

Verse 4   *Repeat Verse 2*

Guitar Chord Songbooks

Each book includes complete lyrics, chord symbols, and guitar chord diagrams.

00701787	Acoustic Hits	$14.99	
00699540	Acoustic Rock	$21.99	
00699914	Alabama	$14.95	
00699566	The Beach Boys	$19.99	
00699562	The Beatles	$17.99	
00702585	Bluegrass	$14.99	
00699648	Johnny Cash	$17.99	
00699539	Children's Songs	$16.99	
00699536	Christmas Carols	$12.99	
00119911	Christmas Songs	$14.99	
00699567	Eric Clapton	$19.99	
00699598	Classic Rock	$18.99	
00703318	Coffeehouse Hits	$14.99	
00699534	Country	$17.99	
00700609	Country Favorites	$14.99	
00140859	Country Hits	$14.99	
00700608	Country Standards	$12.95	
00699636	Cowboy Songs	$19.99	
00701786	Creedence Clearwater Revival	$16.99	
00148087	Jim Croce	$14.99	
00701609	Crosby, Stills & Nash	$16.99	
02501697	John Denver	$17.99	
00700606	Neil Diamond	$19.99	
00295786	Disney	$17.99	
00699888	The Doors	$17.99	
00122917	Eagles	$17.99	
00699916	Early Rock	$14.99	
00699541	Folksongs	$14.99	
00699651	Folk Pop Rock	$17.99	
00115972	40 Easy Strumming Songs	$16.99	
00701611	Four Chord Songs	$14.99	
00702501	Glee	$14.99	
00700463	Gospel Hymns	$14.99	
00699885	Grand Ole Opry®	$16.95	
00139461	Grateful Dead	$14.99	
00103074	Green Day	$14.99	
00701044	Irish Songs	$14.99	
00137847	Michael Jackson	$14.99	
00699632	Billy Joel	$19.99	

00699732	Elton John	$15.99	
00130337	Ray LaMontagne	$12.99	
00700973	Latin Songs	$14.99	
00701043	Love Songs	$14.99	
00701704	Bob Marley	$17.99	
00125332	Bruno Mars	$12.99	
00385035	Paul McCartney	$16.95	
00701146	Steve Miller	$12.99	
00701801	Modern Worship	$16.99	
00699734	Motown	$17.99	
00148273	Willie Nelson	$17.99	
00699762	Nirvana	$16.99	
00699752	Roy Orbison	$17.99	
00103013	Peter, Paul & Mary	$19.99	
00699883	Tom Petty	$15.99	
00139116	Pink Floyd	$14.99	
00699538	Pop/Rock	$16.99	
00699634	Praise & Worship	$14.99	
00699633	Elvis Presley	$17.99	
00702395	Queen	$14.99	
00699710	Red Hot Chili Peppers	$19.99	
00137716	The Rolling Stones	$17.99	
00701147	Bob Seger	$12.99	
00121011	Carly Simon	$14.99	
00699921	Sting	$17.99	
00263755	Taylor Swift	$16.99	
00123860	Three Chord Acoustic Songs	$14.99	
00699720	Three Chord Songs	$17.99	
00119236	Two-Chord Songs	$16.99	
00137744	U2	$14.99	
00700607	Hank Williams	$16.99	
00120862	Stevie Wonder	$14.99	

HAL•LEONARD®

Visit Hal Leonard online at **www.halleonard.com**

Prices, contents, and availability subject to change without notice.

1120
6/9; 116

HAL•LEONARD®
GUITAR
PLAY-ALONG

This series will help you play your favorite songs quickly and easily. Just follow the tab and listen to the CD or online audio to hear how the guitar should sound, and then play along using the separate backing tracks. Playback tools are provided for slowing down the tempo without changing pitch and looping challenging parts. The melody and lyrics are included so that you can sing or simply follow along.

INCLUDES TAB

Complete song lists available online at **halleonard.com**

Availability subject to change without notice.

1120
6/9
051